THE

BASEBALL FANATIC

Books by Louis D. Rubin, Jr.

Babe Ruth's Ghost

Before the Game (photographs by Scott Mylin)

The Curious Death of the Novel

The Edge of the Swamp

The Even-Tempered Angler

The Faraway Country

A Gallery of Southerners

The Golden Weather: A Novel

The Heat of the Sun: A Novel

An Honorable Estate

A Memory of Trains

The Mockingbird in the Gum Tree

My Father's People

Seaports of the South (with J. F. Harrington)

Small Craft Advisory

Surfaces of the Diamond: A Novel

The Teller in the Tale

Thomas Wolfe: The Weather of His Youth

Virginia: A Bicentennial History

The Wary Fugitives

Where the Southern Cross the Yellow Dog

William Elliott Shoots a Bear

The Writer in the South

THE

BASEBALL
FANATIC

The Best Things Ever Said about the
Greatest Game Ever Invented

**Edited with an introduction by
Louis D. Rubin, Jr.**

Foreword by Roy Blount, Jr.

THE LYONS PRESS
Guilford, Connecticut
An imprint of The Globe Pequot Press

Introduction and order copyright © 2000 by Louis D. Rubin, Jr.
Foreword copyright © 2000 by Roy Blount, Jr.

First Lyons Press paperback edition, 2004

The contents of *The Baseball Fanatic* are drawn from *The Quotable
Baseball Fanatic*.

The Lyons Press is an imprint of The Globe Pequot Press.

10 9 8 7 6 5 4 3 2 1

Printed in the United States of America

Designed by Nancy Freeborn | FreebornDesign

ISBN 10: 1-59228-092-7
ISBN 13: 978-1-59228-092-6

10 9 8 7 6 5 4 3 2 1

The Library of Congress has cataloged an earlier hardcover edition
as follows:
The quotable baseball fanatic / compiled by Louis D. Rubin, Jr.,—
1st ed.
     p. cm
  ISBN 1-58574-012-8
   1. Baseball—United States—Quotations, maxims, etc. I.
    Rubin, Louis Decimus, 1923–

GV867.3.Q86 2000
796.357'0973—dc21   99-045877

For Bob Creamer

CONTENTS

FOREWORD

The other day a fact-checker at a magazine called to ask whether the statement "Baseball is a game where people sit around and spit and say stupid things" should, in fact, be attributed to me. Loath as I am to disclaim being the first person to say almost anything, I said no. I did vaguely recall having quoted Bill Lee, the former Red Sox pitcher (that he was a pitcher should go without saying, but you can't say "the former Red Sock"), as having been quoted in the seventies as saying, when asked what he thought about artificial grass, "I don't know, I never smoked any"—that observation had a certain cogency. Coming from a writer, it would be inappropriate. Making clever remarks is not a ballplayer's primary imperative. Before he has any room to talk, he has to speak with bat, ball, fingers, and feet. And yet a player's tongue is often mightier than the pen.

In 1988, when David Cone was a young Met pitcher about to start a crucial play-off game, a more experienced teammate (I'm sorry to say my archives do not record his name) was asked what advice he had given Cone. "There's no magical saying," said the teammate. "There's nothing we can say except he can't look at it like, 'Oh, my God, the earth will crash if I don't do it.' If he realizes the situation too much, that's not good."

That, to me, is wisdom. You have to choose between fully realizing a situation and performing well in it. Or, as Yogi Berra is famously supposed to have said, "You can't think and hit at the same time." Ask anyone who has just pitched a no-hitter or hit a dramatic game-winning home run what the experience was like, and he will tell you, if he is honest, "It hasn't sunk in yet." You have to be a little bit unconcious out there. As Reggie Jackson once said, "When the ball is in the air and it starts hopping, all you can do is follow with your eyes and sing along."

When a ballplayer does come up with an epigram regarding his own play, it likely pertains to poor performance. Once when Reggie was hitting .175, he said, "When you're hitting .175, whatever you say doesn't make much sense." In fact, paradoxically enough, he thereby struck the verbal ball right on the nose. In 1974, when Reggie was at the height of his powers, he sloshed around in the whirlpool bath in the Oakland clubhouse and searched for words to describe what hitting well is like:

"Being in complete control. You have been the dominant force—not the ball, not the pitcher. You have taken over and lined it somewhere." And when the ball goes a long, long ways, "All the baseball players come to rest at that moment and watch you. Everyone is helpless and in awe. . . . And you know it. You're a master. Dealing."

Eloquent in its way, but too far from the general experience of life to have the resonance of something Reggie said in his last season, when asked why he was considering retirement: "I don't want to go on wringing out the rag of ability."

Ballplayers live in a physical world. Joe Morgan is an estimable TV commentator today, but none of his reflections on the fine points of the game have registered with me as distinctly as something he told me once in his prime as a Cincinnati Red, after he hit a line drive into the gap and beat the out-fielder's throw to second by sliding headfirst. "That's the only way I can slide on a double," he said. "Because I be in a deep lean."

Canted profoundly forward, that's the way a ball-player has to be. Acting on faith. Thinking positively, which is not to say scintillatingly. During spring training in 1981 George Foster, newly acquired by the Mets, would respond to questions about the team's prospects by holding his hand over the 5 of the 15 on his chest so that his shirt read "Mets 1." That, he said, was his goal: "If you have a goal, you achieve only twenty percent." Which must mean, a cynical sportswriter observed, that "if you do and you don't, you must achieve a hundred percent." The latter was the sharper remark, but it was also the remark of a man who was not in a deep lean. If you are a ballplayer you do or you don't. Then, somewhat later, you may descend to the level of words.

—Roy Blount, Jr.

INTRODUCTION

In the days of John J. McGraw, when it was considered great to be young and a New York Giant, there
was an umpire named William J. Byron. Known vari-
ously as "Hummingbird," "Lord Byron," and "Singing
Bill," he was a poet and a good baseball man. It was
Byron who, while umpiring in the minors, advised the
Detroit Tigers to sign young Tyrus Raymond Cobb.

In 1913 Byron began a seven-year tenure as a member
of the National League's umpiring staff. Whenever
he made a call that did not meet with the approval
of McGraw and the Giants manager came storming
from the dugout to express his disagreement, as
frequently he did, Byron would burst into song.
"Here comes McGraw!" he sang, to the tune of the
"Bridal Chorus" from *Lohengrin*.

It was Byron's practice sometimes to accompany his decisions on balls and strikes with poetic advice to the batter. "You'll have to learn before you're older/ You can't hit the ball with the bat on your shoulder," he might declare; or, "It cut the middle of the plate/ You missed because you swung too late." Whether his verse was composed on the spur of the moment, or whether it was prepared in advance and applied as occasion arose, is not known, at least not to me.

I cite the above in order to make two points about the book of quotations that follows. They may be best put in the form of questions:

1. In what other team sport is a participant permitted and even expected to make regular visits to the playing field to dispute the judgment of the officials, bringing the game to a complete halt while doing so?

2. How many officials of professional football or basketball games that took place even ten years ago, much less three-quarters of a century, can one identify by name and tell funny stories about?

As must be obvious to all sports fans who do much reading, a great deal that is memorable and interesting about the game of baseball centers on the cultivation of personalities. As Tom Boswell once wrote, "We pretend baseball is primarily a game of teams, when it's more about people. Ted Williams played in only one World Series; Walter Johnson, Hank Aaron and Rogers Hornsby in two each. Who cares or remembers? The team may be the individual's context, but its success is not its definition." What we watch are the members of the teams as they take their separate turns on center stage.

In professional basketball, a sport that requires great skill to play, complex teamwork and split-second screening and positioning are essential to success. Yet unless we happen to be especially experienced observers and at all times know just where to look, most of what we see during a game consists of swift passes and a melee of moving bodies, followed by a Michael Jordan gracefully placing the ball inside the hoop. Contrast that with the spectacle of a pitcher standing in isolation on the mound, getting ready to resume action, taking the sign from the catcher, preparing to throw; and a batter stepping into the box, setting his feet, cocking his wrists and adjusting the hold on his bat, waiting for the pitch. Will it be low and away, in on the fists, or high and outside? Will it be a fastball, a curve, a slider, a changeup? Will it be thrown for a strike, or wasted? There is ample time to observe and anticipate.

The venting of emotion, as noted, is an important part of the spectacle. Those participating are encouraged to sound off. Most of us who have watched televised NFL football games have seen brief footage of this or that coach raging away at a head linesman along the sidelines, while the head linesman totally ignores what is being shouted at him as he prepares for the next play. Let that coach become so irate that he ventures upon the field itself and holds up play, however, and heads will roll, for it is strictly taboo. This may be compared with a Bobby Cox or a Lou Piniella furiously disputing a call at second base, passionately gesturing, the center of all attention, play having been suspended to permit the argument to go on, while the fans in the grandstand are vigorously expressing their own opinions. The difference in conduct and mores is beyond dispute.

To that, add the number of baseball games played during a season, the number of separate appearances in action, and the number of years in which a good player can remain in public view, and it is not difficult to see why the sport is dominated by its personalities, and why the antics of individuals are so much a part of the game and its history. This is why we remember, and can quote so specifically, what has been said by and about them, and about the game they play.

The book that follows is based on that fundamental fact, and is made up of comments by persons who have been involved in professional baseball, whether as participants, commentators, or simply as spectators. Some are humorous, others not so. I do not say that a similar book might not be assembled from sayings and writings about other major sports, but surely there would be many fewer quotations from which to choose.

There is a famous comment by F. Scott Fitzgerald to the effect that Ring Lardner's muse was permanently constrained by the boundaries of Frank Chance's diamond, the implication being that had Lardner not spent his formative years covering baseball in Chicago and listening to the conversations of athletes, the fiction he later wrote would have been more ambitious, of greater range, and more richly imaginative—i.e., more like Fitzgerald's.

Jonathan Yardley, for one, has disputed this, on the grounds that no good purpose was served by trying to make Lardner into a different and supposedly more artistically ennobled kind of writer than what he so felicitously was. Surely this is true. The real question is not whether Lardner might have written to greater literary purpose if he had spent his late teens and early twenties in an environment offering greater intellectual stimulation than a dugout or a press box. It is why the game of baseball could exercise so powerful a hold on his youthful imagination, and in the particular form that it did.

Whatever the reasons, it cannot be denied that major league baseball has engaged the attention of a number of very talented writers. It would appear to provide, for some of them, a kind of bridge between what is intellectually and artistically sophisticated on the one hand, and what is exciting and appealing to a mass general audience on the other. I do not mean by this that the other major sports have no appeal for the intelligentsia; clearly they do. But for whatever reason, when the urge to write about such things comes along, it is usually baseball that they choose to write about.

I sometimes think that no small portion of the fascination of reading about baseball arises from the contrast between the way in which the game is written about by its literary admirers, and the way it is talked about by its player personnel. This is particularly true for humor. If, as has been maintained, incongruity is what lies at the root of all comedy, then consider the difference in levels of discourse displayed in so much that appears in this book. It may be seen beginning with the first section, entitled "On the

Game." Whose insight comes closer to the unadulterated truth about the innermost nature of the National Game, the noted former practitioner Yogi Berra's, or the distinguished philosopher Morris R. Cohen's? The answer, of course, is that both comments are much to the point.

Baseball players can be and frequently are very witty. With only very rare exceptions, however, they display their wit in conversation, not on paper. When their names appear on book jackets, it is habitually in company with someone else's, "as told to," or "with" another person; in other words, the books are the work of ghostwriters.

"As told to" books are principally aimed at the young adult audience, and one can never be sure that the ballplayer actually said or even thought what he has supposedly written. Most such books are eminently forgettable. Not so the first-person memoirs of a relatively new subgenre invented by Lawrence Ritter and since practiced by Donald Honig, Anthony Connor, Daniel Peary, and numerous others. What Ritter had the inspiration to do, back in the 1960s, was to track down and interview a number of old-time ballplayers, and develop their spoken memories into first-person sketches. At the time he did this, not only were some of the stars of the Dead Ball Era still around, but even a few who had played the game professionally back before the turn of the twentieth century.

The Glory of Their Times is a deceptive book. So skillfully have the random and sometimes discordant replies of the old-timers been woven into seamless narratives that a reader might think that Ritter did little more than take down their recollections. In actuality it is Ritter who provides most of the development, the cohesion and the continuity. Not all his emulators have been as successful.

Some of the very best writing about baseball is in biographies: Robert Creamer's *Stengel*, Murray Polner's *Branch Rickey*, Peter Williams on Bill Terry's career, and so on. Columnists such as George F. Will and Thomas Boswell likewise produce felicitous prose, the best of which has been collected and published, while Roger Angell's extensive *New*

Yorker commentaries are imaginative and frequently eloquent.

On the other hand, a great deal of baseball writing is flat, sterile stuff, composed on the stylistic level of the Horatio Alger tales. For every craftsman of the language such as Roger Kahn and Leonard Koppett, there are numerous authors of baseball books which read as if their prose was bolted into place on an assembly line. Some of the worst baseball writing comes from the "as told to" books written for the young adult trade, which seek to convey the impression that the ballplayer himself is actually doing the writing through attempting to counterfeit his vocabulary, four-letter words and all. I could quote examples, but it would be too depressing. Still, ghostwriting can be also spritely and deft, as witness the job that Ed Linn did for and on Leo Durocher in *Nice Guys Finish Last*.

In part, the liveliness of a baseball book depends upon the particular subject matter. Obviously an author who writes of Casey Stengel or Ty Cobb has an inherent advantage over one who chronicles Joe

DiMaggio or Rogers Hornsby, in that the latter two, for all their talent with a baseball bat, have little to offer in the way of personality. DiMaggio was aloof and inchoate, while Hornsby was a sourpuss, and a biographer's language can do only so much to atone for a subject's lack of color. Even so, writers choose their own subjects, and those with a feel for prose tend to write books about interesting ballplayers. It is also a fact that an extremely useful qualification for writing baseball books is a sense of humor, which unfortunately not all who have done so possess.

To select the quotations that make up this book, I read, or more usually reread, several hundred books, and picked the brains of various knowledgeable acquaintances. I tried, so far as was possible, to avoid some of the more time-worn quotations, such as Ping Bodie's announcement that he roomed with Babe Ruth's suitcase, or Dizzy Dean's comment that if he had known that his brother Paul was going to pitch a no-hitter, he would have done the same, and the like. On the other hand, I could not bring myself to leave out, for example, Bugs Baer on Bodie's feet being more law-abiding than his intentions, and sometimes I deliberately included a platitude because it was and is so obviously that. Thus I cited Jacques Barzun's oft-quoted comment about whoever would know the mind and heart of America needing to study baseball, which is so regularly invoked in order to justify the importance of a game that needs no justification. As well contend that whoever would know the mind and heart of America must know peanut butter.

Writing and thinking about baseball is always subject to the temptations of nostalgia. Not only is the game played during one's childhood and youth, and thus recollected with the fondness for a period when the future still appeared open for the taking, but the time for playing and watching baseball was usually the summertime, when school was out and the sky high and blue. For this and other reasons the Good Old Days, and the resulting legend of Decline and Fall, have constituted a thriving dimension of the game for more than a century now. The seemingly valid specificity and continuity of baseball statistics, as contrasted with those of other sports, helps to feed the myth of the Golden Age. How could even the best of today's pitchers compare favorably with a Christy Mathewson, who won 37 games, with an earned run average of 1.43, and completed 34 games in 1908? The fact that the statistics are only relatively comparable, and that there are a number of reasons why pitching major league baseball is a far more difficult affair today, matters little when viewed through the lens of the Search for Lost Time. Just when the Golden Age was at its zenith depends upon one's own antiquity. Not many old timers have the objectivity of Wilbert Robinson when asked to compare the New York Yankees of the 1920s with the fabled Orioles of the 1890s. "They would have kicked the hell out of us," Uncle Robbie declared, to the indignation of John McGraw and others of his old Baltimore teammates.

One of the earliest pieces about baseball that I read was by Robert Benchley, in a collection of his magazine pieces entitled *Love Conquers All* (1922). I read it in the mid-1930s. Benchley was suggesting, facetiously, that baseball fans should have a distinctive dress, as follows: "Straw hat, worn well back on the head; one cigar, unlighted, held between teeth; vest worn but unbuttoned and open, displaying both a belt and suspenders, with gold watchchain connecting the bottom pockets."

Obviously the fan is wearing a suit, with a vest, and almost nobody would dress so formally and cumbrously for baseball games any more. Pocket watches and chains have virtually disappeared, in favor of wristwatches. Suspenders are for the most part long gone. It is taboo to smoke cigars in public, and nobody would buy one at today's prices merely to chew on it. The straw hat alone remains valid, and then only for some. Moreover, it was Benchley's assumption that a baseball fan was by definition male; another sketch in the same collection contains a humorous portrayal of the sufferings of a husband who makes the mistake of taking his wife along to a Yankees game. She cannot understand, for example, why a base runner coming home does not constitute a home run.

So the comedy in Benchley's piece, based as it is on "typical" diamond-watching garb as popularly portrayed in the early 1920s, is almost totally outdated.

But what was taking place not in the grandstand but out on the playing field then has in most respects changed very little. As A. Bartlett Giamatti has said, the game's rules were established, "with almost no exceptions of consequence, by 1895." In essence, its fundamentals do remain the same.

Thus, what Burleigh Grimes, one of the last of the legal spitballers, quotes Rogers Hornsby coming out to the mound and telling him at a crucial point of a game played some seven decades ago could be spoken by any manager of any era: "Don't give him anything good, but don't walk him." And the perennially unfeeling ways of numerous bleacherites toward once-lustrous veterans grown old and slow were amply summed up by a comment made to me by a spectator at a minor league game in Baltimore forty-seven years ago. "Baseball fans," he remarked, "have short memories. I've even seen them boo Walter Johnson, and in my opinion he was the greatest pitcher who ever lived."

The fans too can be long-suffering, however. It was so in Mudville, and in Cleveland, Chicago, Atlanta,

Boston, and everywhere else that the game has been played. I once did a tabulation designed to indicate which major league city's fans have suffered most and least over the years, in the way of having to get by without home teams in the pennant races. Counting the annual records of all but the most recent franchises, I found, not surprisingly, that from 1901 through the 1995 season a baseball fan living in New York City was most likely to have a local team finish the season fewer than ten games out of the running. By contrast, a fan living in Philadelphia, whether rooting for the Phillies or, before 1955, the Athletics, was least apt of all to have enjoyed such a privilege—less so, even, than a citizen of Chicago.

Still, pain can be inflicted by any ball team anywhere upon its adherents. I doubt that a more difficult time, more demanding of fortitude and calling for greater spiritual resolve, was ever endured than was true for partisans of the then–New York Giants on the day, midway through the 1948 season, when the news came that Mel Ott had been fired as manager and Leo Durocher hired in his stead. By definition all Giant fans adored Ott. Contrariwise, they did not merely dislike Leo; they hated him with a passion. It was Leo who had snarled and cursed and hustled the Dodgers along to hegemony among National League teams in New York City following almost forty years of Giant dominance. It was he who had pointed to Mel Ott and the Giants and declared that nice guys finished last. Ottie was a gentleman, Durocher a barroom brawler, crude and mannerless. And now he, of all people, was being placed in charge of the Giants!

The New York papers were full of the news. The views of various fans were solicited. There were those patrons of the Polo Grounds who declared that this was the end. They could take no more. They were cancelling lifelong allegiances. It was a fan of the Brooklyn Dodgers, however, who came up with what to my mind was one of the classic baseball utterances of all time. I have remembered it ever since. "Jeez!" he declared. "It's Poil Harbor for da Giants!" Yet as it turned out, the Polo Grounds regulars were soon to relent, and three seasons later Leo's Giants won the pennant.

The book that follows divides roughly into two parts. The first consists of comments appropriate to certain general topics and attitudes, as for example the On the Game, the On the Old Days, the art of catching, the end of the color line, sports writers, and so on. The second part contains remarks about or by various players of the game. Little attempt has been made to "cover" all the best-known or most representative players. While at work on this book I focused on finding piquant comments rather than any treatment of particular subjects. The groupings came afterward. Some may wonder why, for example, there are five pages of quotations having to do with Ty Cobb, but none about Harry Heilman or Al Simmons. It is because I don't know of, and didn't in my readings happen to come across, striking comments by or about either of the latter two gentlemen, remarkable though their hitting skills were, while almost everybody had something to say, frequently derogatory, about the Georgia Peach.

So it goes in what has been described as "the temple of baseball," but that to my mind has always seemed more like a high-quality three-ring circus.

—L. D. R.
  Chapel Hill, North Carolina
  May 11, 1999

ON
THE GAME

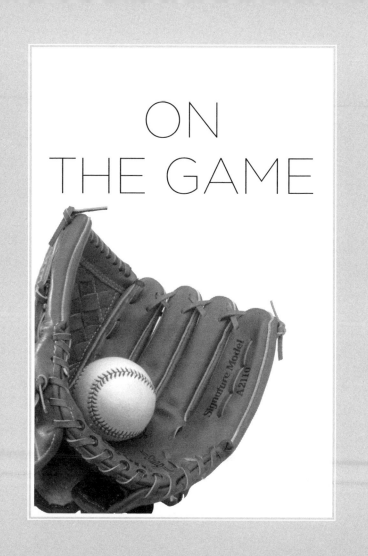

Brains are as much a necessity in base-ball as in any other profession. The best ball players are the most intelligent, though, of course, natural intelligence is here meant and not necessarily that which is derived from books.

—JOHN MONTGOMERY WARD
PITCHER, INFIELDER, OUTFIELDER,
1878–1894; MANAGER, SEVEN
SEASONS, 1880–1894; OWNER, 1912;
HALL OF FAME

Critics who spurn baseball as slow and tranquil, out of step with the violence which mars our times, fail to grasp its enormous impact on the masses. Baseball's solitary grace is not obscured in a bedlam of bodies, or in a jarring crash near the goal, or in a madcap scramble near the backboard. Its grace exists to be seen, not clouded, and those who excel on the field or in the broadcast booth magnify that artistry.

—CURT SMITH
SPORTSWRITER, BASEBALL
BIOGRAPHER

I love baseball too much to do anything else. When the season is over I'm grouchy all the time. I feel miserable. I'm always sick. I get imaginary pains, like a baby. Only when spring training comes around and I can put the uniform back on do the pains go away.

—WOODY HUYKE
SCOUT

When my revered friend and teacher William James wrote an essay on "A Moral Equivalent for War," I suggested to him that baseball already embodied all the moral value of war, so far as war had any moral value. He listened sympathetically and was amused, but he did not take me seriously enough. All great men have their limitations, and William James's were due to the fact that he lived in Cambridge, a city which, in spite of the fact that it has a population of 100,000 souls (including the professors), is not represented in any baseball league that can be detected without a microscope.

—MORRIS R. COHEN
LEGAL PHILOSOPHER

Before a game in St. Louis in 1955, Russ [Meyer] was sitting alone in the Dodgers dugout. He picked up an old baseball, looked at it carefully, and said, speaking to himself and to no one: "Just think of it. This little ball causes all of the trouble."

—JAMES T. FARRELL
NOVELIST

Midsummer baseball feels as if it would last forever; late-season baseball becomes quicker and terser, as if sensing its coming end, and sometimes, if we are lucky, it explodes into brilliant terminal colors, leaving bright pictures in memory to carry us through the miserable months to come.

—ROGER ANGELL
AUTHOR, EDITOR

For someone whose roots in America were strong but only inches deep, and who had no experience, such as a Catholic child might, of an awesome hierarchy that was real and felt, baseball was a kind of secular church that reached into every class and region of the nation and bound millions upon millions of us together in common concerns, loyalties, rituals, enthusiasms, and antagonisms. Baseball made me understand what patriotism was about, at its best.

—PHILIP ROTH
NOVELIST

I claim that Base Ball owes its prestige as our National Game to the fact that as no other sport it is the exponent of American Courage, Confidence, Combativeness; American Dash, Discipline, Determination; American Energy, Eagerness, Enthusiasm; American Pluck, Persistency, Performance; American Spirit, Sagacity, Success; American Vim, Vigor, Virility.

—ALBERT G. SPALDING
PITCHER, OUTFIELDER, 1871–1878;
MANAGER, 1876–1877; OWNER,
1882–1891; HALL OF FAME

Genteel in its origins, proletarian in its development, egalitarian in its demands and appeal, effortless in its adaptation to nature, raucous, hard-nosed, and glamorous as a profession, expanding with the country like fingers unfolding from a fist, image of a lost past, evergreen reminder of America's best promises, baseball fits America.

—A. BARTLETT GIAMATTI
UNIVERSITY PROFESSOR,
PRESIDENT; PRESIDENT,
NATIONAL LEAGUE, 1986–1989;
COMMISSIONER OF BASEBALL,
1989–1992

It ain't like football.
You can't make up
no trick plays.

—YOGI BERRA
CATCHER, 1946–1965; 358 HOME
RUNS; MANAGER, 1964, 1972–1975,
1984–1985; COACH; HALL OF FAME

It's great to be young and
a Giant.

—LARRY DOYLE
INFIELDER, 1907-1920

If you became a Yankee, you took on the quality of breeding which the Yankees exemplified. You became a Yankee, and that answered a whole lot of questions. For some reason you were able to perform a little better.

—WAITE HOYT
PITCHER, 1918–1927; WON 237 GAMES LIFETIME; SPORTSCASTER; HALL OF FAME

Of all the teams I played on, the Yankees were the team that drank the most.

—JOE DE MAESTRI

INFIELDER, 1951–1961

With exceptions like Oakland and the pennant-winning Yankee teams I played on (where there was more dissention than on my last-place Seattle Pilots), winning teams tend to have less dis-sention because players having good years are generally happier. Dissention is the result, rather than the cause, of losing.

—JIM BOUTON
PITCHER, 1962–1970, 1978: AUTHOR

Baseball isn't a life-and-death matter, but the Red Sox are.

—MIKE BARNICLE
SPORTSWRITER

Those Dodger-Giant games weren't baseball. They were civil war.

—ANDY PAFKO

OUTFIELDER, 1943–1959

Wee Willie Keeler
Runs through the town,
All along Charles Street
In his night gown,
Belling like a hound dog
Gathering the pack:
Hello, Wilbert Robinson,
The Orioles are back!

—OGDEN NASH
POET

When I read a ball player saying he doesn't hear the boos, I think one thing: "The Hell You Don't."

—PEE WEE REESE
INFIELDER, 16 SEASONS,
1940–1958; HALL OF FAME

Don't believe the benched player who insists he is content "as long as my team wins." That dog won't hunt.

—TIM McCARVER
CATCHER, 1959–1980;
SPORTSCASTER; SPORTSWRITER

But baseball is a very humbling game. Just when you think you are on top and feel like you are big and nobody can get you out, you go into a slump and everybody gets you out.

—BERNIE WILLIAMS
OUTFIELDER, 1991–

Baseball's great appeal lies in the combination of anticipation and accomplishment: what might happen and then what does happen, either way. Mantle at bat was the epitome of this: the tension as he cocked his bat and the pitcher prepared to throw. He might strike out—an explosive, breath-deflating moment—or he might belt one—to roaring exultation from the stands.

—ROBERT W. CREAMER
SPORTSWRITER, BIOGRAPHER,
EDITOR

With the same amount of natural common sense behind him, the college boy has a full two years' jump on the town-lot boy.

The difference is simply this—the college boy, or anyone with even a partially trained mind, immediately tries to find his faults; the unschooled fellow usually tries to hide his.

—JOHN McGRAW

INFIELDER, 1891–1906;
.344 LIFETIME BATTING AVERAGE;
MANAGER, 33 YEARS, 1899–1932;
WON TEN PENNANTS, THREE
WORLD SERIES; HALL OF FAME

I don't like college boys.

—TIM HURST

**AFTER AN ARGUMENT IN WHICH,
AS AN UMPIRE, HE ALLEGEDLY
SPAT IN EDDIE COLLINS'S FACE**

What a way to make a living! I even enjoyed those long train rides, swinging back and forth across the country. I'd sit by the window and watch the farmland and small towns pass by, and now and then see a Model-T tooling along the country roads. You didn't see too many cars back then, especially in the boondocks.

—LES BELL

INFIELDER, 1923–31

We would leave Boston at five o'clock in the afternoon. Ride all night, all the next day, till eleven o'clock at night to get to St. Louis. Then play a game the next day. No air-conditioning. Windows wide open. Coal dust flying in your face. I'd like to see these guys today, with their salaries, try to play ball with all that.

—LES TIETJE
PITCHER, 1933–1938

Whoever would know the mind and heart of America had better learn baseball . . .

—JACQUES BARZUN
ROMANCE LANGUAGES SCHOLAR

Some people even
claim that ballplayers
are human.

—JIM BROSNAN

PITCHER, NINE SEASONS,
1954–1963; AUTHOR;
SPORTSCASTER

Just the other day a fellow wrote how I'd tear into home plate with my spikes high as if I intended to cut the catcher in half. What he didn't mention was that the catcher would put his mask in front of the plate, and the bat, too, if he had time to reach for it. Paul Kritchell of the Browns did that once too often.

. . . I slid in high, scissored him between my legs, a bone snapped in his shoulder and the guy never caught another ball game in his life.

—TY COBB
OUTFIELDER, 1905–1928; LIFETIME
BATTING AVERAGE .366; LED
LEAGUE IN HITTING 12 SEASONS;
892 STOLEN BASES; MANAGER,
1921–1926; HALL OF FAME

Any kind of reputation if it's mean is not bad to have in baseball.

—LEW BURDETTE
PITCHER, 1950–1967;
WON 203 GAMES

Kid, when you kick a water bucket you don't kick it with your toe. Use the side of your foot. Okay?

—LEFTY GROVE
PITCHER, 1925–1941; WON 300
GAMES, .680 WINNING
PERCENTAGE; HALL OF FAME.
TO A ROOKIE PITCHER WHO
BROKE HIS BIG TOE KICKING A
WATER BUCKET IN ANGER

They cannot beat us.
Am en route.

—BLONDY RYAN

INFIELDER, SIX SEASONS,
1930–1938, TELEGRAM TO
1933 NEW YORK GIANTS

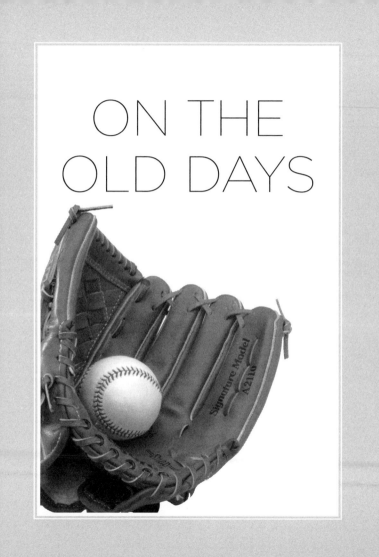

ON THE
OLD DAYS

I have read so much about the old-timers and heard older players and writers and fans (including my father) talk about them so often that they are almost as visible to me as the stars I have watched on the field.

—ROGER ANGELL
AUTHOR, EDITOR

Whenever the ball is caught after rebounding from the side of a building, a fence, or a tree, provided it has touched the ground but once, it should be considered a fair catch, unless a special arrangement to the contrary be made previous to the commencement of the match. This rule will also hold good in the case of a catch without touching the ground at all.

—SEYMOUR R. CHURCH
SPORTSWRITER, LATE 19TH TO EARLY 20TH CENTURY

In fact, "modern" baseball ought to be dated not from the beginning of the twentieth century, as popular lore confidently assumes, but from the season of 1893. Under the new rules, the pitching distance was lengthened from fifty feet to sixty feet, six inches; the rectangular pitcher's box was eliminated; and, as he delivered the ball to the batter, the pitcher was required to keep his back foot anchored to a twelve-by-four rubber slab (enlarged to twenty-four by six inches in 1895.) The results were everything the rule-makers could have desired. The 1893 season brought the sharpest increase in batting figures in the sport's history: a thirty-five-point rise in the overall National League average and almost a thousand more runs.

—CHARLES C. ALEXANDER
BASEBALL HISTORIAN,
BIOGRAPHER

Names like Whitey, Hoss, Brickyard, Dapper Dan, and Big Bill are easily understood, and we can guess how Benny (Earache) Meyer earned his designation. We can guess why Dirty Jack Doyle played for twelve different teams in seventeen years, too. Since he won 203 games, Al Orth (1895–1909) probably didn't mind being called "the Curveless Wonder," but what did Bill Lattimore do in his four-game stay with the 1908 Cleveland club to earn the title "Slothful Bill"? And how, in God's name, did Hub Perdue, of the Boston Braves and St. Louis Cardinals (1911–15) come to be called "the Gallatin Squash"*?

—ART HILL
SPORTSWRITER

[* ans.—because he came from Gallatin, Missouri, and was shaped like a squash.—ed.]

In St. Louis, the Browns would assemble at Von der Ahe's saloon and march down to Sportsman's Park. A silk-hatted, swaggering Chris would lead the formation, flanked by his two sleek greyhounds, Snoozer and Schnauser. Chris would beam as he acknowledged cheers, but he was always bewildered by the laughter that followed him. Had he ever bothered to look back, Chris would have seen third baseman [Arlie] Latham aping the Boss's gait and wearing a bright red false nose reminiscent of Chris's bulbous proboscis.

—RICHARD EGENRIETHER
LIBRARIAN, BASEBALL HISTORIAN

Indeed, racism and anti-Semitism turn up in the sports pages of the era [the 1900s] in ways that would now be considered shocking. It is sobering to realize that prejudice and bigotry were evidently as American as apple pie back in those idyllic "good old days of yesteryear."

—LAWRENCE RITTER
**BASEBALL HISTORIAN,
UNIVERSITY PROFESSOR**

As a mascot the Boston brigade had an aged darky along, and when the band played "Dixie" the old chap capered nimbly on the roof of the Boston team's bench. When the band played "Old Black Joe" he moved back and forth with measured tread.

—*NEW YORK SUN*, OCTOBER 11, 1904

Doubtless the preponderance of hayseeds has been exaggerated . . . but essentially it was a country boys' game played by hillbillies and urban rejects. They simply happened to have a talent for hitting a ball with a bat or throwing a curve, and in many cases it was the only talent they had. A few collegians gave a veneer of social respectability to their ranks, but many players were illiterate, coarse, and incredibly naive. A great deal of heavy drinking went on, much of it induced by the boredom of life on the road and the eagerness of worshipful fans to ply their heroes with hard liquor.

—JONATHAN YARDLEY
AUTHOR, BOOK CRITIC

No member of the team while dressed in his uniform shall be permitted to flirt with or 'mash' any female or lady.

—PHILADELPHIA ATHLETICS CLUB RULES, 1883

When he quit the League umpiring staff in midseason 1895, onetime Giants pitching star Tim Keefe described baseball as having become "absolutely disagreeable. It is the fashion now for every player to froth at the mouth and emit shrieks of anguish whenever a decision is given which is adverse to the interests of the club."

—CHARLES C. ALEXANDER
**BASEBALL HISTORIAN,
BIOGRAPHER**

Actually, there was very little drinking in baseball in those days.

—RUBE MARQUARD

HALL OF FAME PITCHER,

NEW YORK GIANTS, 1908–1925

In [the] dead-ball era, a complete game required perhaps half the number of pitches required today. And with little danger of a home run by any but the very best batters, pitchers didn't have to bear down as hard on every pitch, the way they do today. In short, they pitched more often because they didn't work as hard when they worked.

—LEONARD KOPPETT
SPORTSWRITER, EDITOR

Bill Veeck's midget, Eddie Gaedel, of course, was the lightest player of all time. It seems unlikely that any professional of the future will weigh less than his 65 pounds.

—LEE ALLEN

**SPORTSWRITER,
CURATOR OF HALL OF FAME**

Hall of Fame shortstop Rabbit Maranville committed 65 errors for the 1914 Miracle Braves; 70 years later Alan Trammell had 10 for the world champion Tigers.

—JIM KAPLAN
SPORTSWRITER, AUTHOR

There's no doubt in my mind that the old-time ballplayer was smarter than the modern player. No doubt at all. That's what baseball was all about then, a game of strategy and tactics, and if you played in the Big Leagues you had to know how to think, and think quick, or you'd be back in the minors before you knew what in the world hit you.

—SAM CRAWFORD
OUTFIELDER, 1899–1917;
1,525 RBI; HALL OF FAME

To think that so small a man as Keeler should lead all the League sluggers! Truly it is the eye and not the size.

—*SPORTING LIFE* (1895)

Giants have not ceded to mere mortals. I'll bet anything that [Rod] Carew could match [Willie] Keeler. Rather, the boundaries of baseball have been drawn in and its edges smoothed. The game has achieved a grace and precision of execution that has, as one effect, eliminated the extreme achievements of early years. A game unmatched for style and detail has simply become more balanced and beautiful.

—STEPHEN JAY GOULD
SCIENTIST, AUTHOR

A lot of people will tell you that the modern player can't compare to the old timer. Not even in the same league, they say. Well, maybe they're right, but I don't think so. I don't think there's ever been a better outfielder than Willie Mays, or a better left-handed pitcher than Sandy Koufax, or a better third baseman than Brooks Robinson, just to name three that are playing today.

—AL BRIDWELL
INFIELDER, 1905–1915

They would have kicked
the hell out of us.

—WILBERT ROBINSON
CATCHER, 1886–1902; MANAGER,
1902, 1914–1931; HALL OF FAME,
ASKED TO COMPARE THE
YANKEES OF THE 1920s WITH
THE BALTIMORE ORIOLES OF
HIS OWN DAY

ON
LOSERS

Of the sixteen teams that existed in 1949, all have since won league championships—all but the Cubs. And which of the old National League teams was first to finish in tenth place behind even the expansion teams? Don't ask.

—GEORGE F. WILL
COLUMNIST

One dreary afternoon [in the 1930s], Dave Driscoll, business manager of the Dodgers, was walking in Philadelphia and chanced to pass Baker Bowl. The Phillies were on the road, but in spite of that a pathetic vendor of peanuts was hawking his wares before an imaginary crowd near the entrance to the bleachers.

"There won't be a crowd here today," Driscoll told him. "Why don't you go to Shibe Park [where the Athletics were playing that day]?"

"I've been to Shibe Park," the vendor replied. "There's nobody there either."

—LEE ALLEN
SPORTSWRITER,
CURATOR OF HALL OF FAME

The trouble is, we are in a losing streak at the wrong time. If we were losing like this in the middle of the season, nobody would notice. But we are losing at the beginning of the season [1962, the Mets' first year], and this sets up the possibility of losing all 162 games.

—CASEY STENGEL
OUTFIELDER, 1912–1925; MANAGER,
1934–1943, 1949–1960, 1962–1965;
WON TEN PENNANTS, SEVEN
WORLD SERIES, FIVE IN A ROW;
COACH; HALL OF FAME

Come out and see my Amazin' Mets. I been in the game a hundred years but I see new ways to lose I never knew existed before.

—CASEY STENGEL

We was going to get you a birthday cake, but we figured you'd drop it.

—CASEY STENGEL

I tell you what: I'm going to put in a pinch hitter for you because I don't want you to tie the record.

—CONNIE MACK
CATCHER. 1886-1896; MANAGER. 53 SEASONS. 1894-1950; WON EIGHT PENNANTS, FIVE WORLD SERIES; HALL OF FAME.
AFTER EDDIE JOOST HAD BEEN STRUCK OUT THREE TIMES BY BOB FELLER

When all is said and done, all I want anyone to say of me is, "Earl Weaver— he sure was a good sore loser."

—EARL WEAVER
MANAGER, 1968–1982, 1985–1986;
SIX FIRST PLACE FINISHES,
WON ONE WORLD SERIES;
HALL OF FAME

With Bob Gibson, it wasn't that he wanted to win so much as that he didn't want to lose. He hated to lose. He just couldn't accept it.

—TIM McCARVER
CATCHER, 1959–1980;
SPORTSCASTER; SPORTSWRITER

The nice guys are all over there [in the Giants dugout]. In last place.

—LEO DUROCHER
INFIELDER, 17 YEARS, 1925–1945;
MANAGER, 24 YEARS. 1939–1973;
WON THREE PENNANTS, ONE
WORLD SERIES;
HALL OF FAME

The sun don't shine on the same dog's ass all the time.

—CATFISH HUNTER
PITCHER, 1965–1979; WON 224 GAMES LIFETIME; HALL OF FAME, AFTER LOSING TO THE DODGERS, 6–1, IN THE 1977 WORLD SERIES.

What a hell of a league this is. I hit
.387, .408, and .395 the last three
years and I ain't won nothin' yet.

SHOELESS JOE JACKSON
OUTFIELDER, 1908–1920; LIFETIME
BATTING AVERAGE .358; BANNED
FROM GAME FOR LIFETIME IN
BLACK SOX SCANDAL

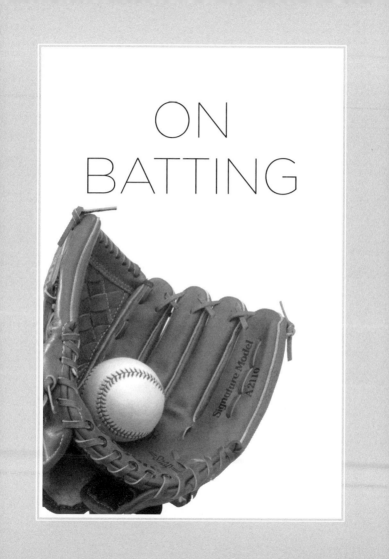

ON
BATTING

Always have a belligerent, take-charge attitude up there. You have to cultivate quite a "mad on" while awaiting your turn at bat, a cold determination to ram the ball down the pitcher's throat. You'd be surprised how effective it is.

—TY COBB
OUTFIELDER, 1905–1928; LIFETIME
BATTING AVERAGE .366; LED
LEAGUE IN HITTING 12 SEASONS;
892 STOLEN BASES; MANAGER,
1921–1926; HALL OF FAME

Keep your eye clear and
hit 'em where they ain't.

—WEE WILLIE KEELER
OUTFIELDER, 1892–1909;
LIFETIME BATTING AVERAGE .341;
HALL OF FAME

A good leadoff hitter is a pain
in the ass to pitchers.

—RICHIE ASHBURN
OUTFIELDER 1948–1962; LIFETIME
.308 HITTER, DEFENSIVE STAR;
HALL OF FAME

I was playing in a game in St. Louis in 1917. [George] Sisler hit one along the ground. I run in and scoop it up. But I don't throw the ball. I hold it. There were ten perforations in it, one, two, three, four, ten perforations. I ran to the umpire and said he had better look at Sisler's bat. He had driven nails in it and filed them down.

—BUCK WEAVER
INFIELDER, 1912–1920;
BANNED FROM GAME FOR LIFE
IN BLACK SOX SCANDAL

[Wilcy Moore] had the perfect stance at the plate and the perfect swing. The only trouble was that he always swung in the same spot, no matter where the ball was, so that if he hit it, it was by accident. Ruth, after one look at him in batting practice at the training camp, bet him $300 to $100 that he wouldn't make three hits all season. He made five. When he got home he wrote the Babe a letter.

"The $300 come in handy," it said. "I used it to buy a fine pair of mules. I named one Babe and the other Ruth."

—FRANK GRAHAM
SPORTSWRITER

One day a batter—I believe it was Duane Kuiper—struck out against Catfish Hunter on three magnificent pitches on the outside corner. He didn't swing at any of them. After I called him out on the third pitch he just shook his head and said, "That's the problem with these bats today. They're just not making wood the way they used to."

—RON LUCIANO
UMPIRE, 1968–1980; AUTHOR

You'll have to learn before
you're older

You can't hit the ball with the
bat on your shoulder.

—BILL BYRON

LONGTIME UMPIRE, MAJORS
1913–1919: "THE SINGING UMPIRE"

"The legs go first." That's one of the most universal sports clichés. Obviously, it does not apply to hitters. What goes first, as a man ages, is the hair-trigger reflex needed to control the bat properly—and, at just about the same time, the confidence in one's dodging reflex. Most players would never admit it, and some perhaps don't even realize it, but when a man reaches a certain age (or a certain state of satisfaction), the fear he originally conquered comes back.

—LEONARD KOPPETT
SPORTSWRITER, EDITOR

You decide you'll wait for your pitch. As the ball starts toward the plate, you think about your stance. And then you think about your swing. Then you realize that the ball that went by you for a strike was your pitch.

—BOBBY MURCER,
OUTFIELDER, 1965–1983

When a [Samurai] warrior killed himself, he needed an assistant who would finish the job by cutting his head off. The task was always left to a trusted and highly skilled swordsman, because this had to be done with one clean, perfect stroke. If the stroke was not perfect, the result would be a horrible mess. I approached the task of hitting a baseball in the same manner.

—SADAHARU OH
    JAPANESE BASEBALL STAR;
    HIT 858 HOME RUNS

I enjoyed hitting. I just didn't make contact too often.

—BOB BUHL

PITCHER, 1953–1967; LIFETIME
MAJOR LEAGUE BATTING
RECORD 76 FOR 857

If you're a major league ball player, you ought to have pride. Learn to stroke outside pitches to the opposite field. That's part of your job. A major league hitter is supposed to be a professional.

—STAN MUSIAL
OUTFIELDER, INFIELDER, 22
SEASONS, 1941–1963; .331 LIFETIME
BATTING AVERAGE: 475 HOME
RUNS; HALL OF FAME

[Hank Aaron] had great forearms and wrists. He could be fooled completely and be way out on his front foot and the bat would still be back and he'd just roll his wrists and hit the ball out of the ballpark.

—LEW BURDETTE
PITCHER, 1950–1967;
WON 203 GAMES

I've seen many a fellow who chased himself right back to the minor leagues because he just wouldn't choke up his bat.

—SMOKY JOE WOOD
PITCHER, OUTFIELDER,
14 YEARS, 1909–1922

ON THE LONG BALL

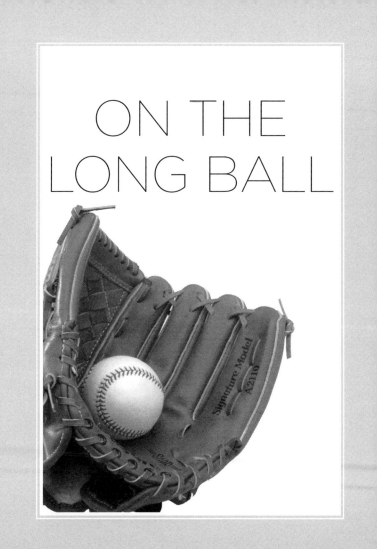

. . . that rutting class of slugging bats-men who think of nothing else when they go to bat but that of gaining the applause of the "groundlings" by the novice's hit to the outfield of a "homer," one of the least difficult hits known to batting in baseball, as it needs only muscle and not brains to make it.

—*SPALDING BASEBALL GUIDE*, 1886

I mean, it's unheard of for somebody to hit 70 home runs. I'm slightly in awe of myself.

—MARK McGWIRE
INFIELDER. 1986– ; SET NEW
RECORD OF 70 HOME RUNS IN 1998

Imagine, if you will, that the two players chasing Maris and Babe Ruth had been Albert Belle and Barry Bonds. People might still have paid attention—the way you pay attention to a car wreck.

—STEVE ASCHBURNER
SPORTSWRITER

This summer (1977), a left-hand-swinging half-Chinese thirty-seven-year-old slugger named Sadaharu Oh struck the seven-hundred-and-fifty-sixth home run of his career, while playing for the Yomiuri Giants in Japan, and thus surpassed (in a way) Hank Aaron's lifetime mark; the qualifying parenthesis suggests that Japanese ballparks and Japanese pitchers are not all of major-league dimensions—a fact that the wonderful Oh admitted when he politely murmured, "I don't think I would do as well in American baseball."

—ROGER ANGELL
AUTHOR, EDITOR

This isn't life or death. We're like those surfer dudes out on the ocean. When you get up on a good wave, you ride it out as long as you can.

—BARRY BONDS
OUTFIELDER, 1986

ON BASE
RUNNING

A defensive play is at least five times as hard to make as an offensive play. An error by a fielder can come from a bad throw, a bad hop of the ball, the muff of an easy chance, the ball hitting the runner or a mix-up in responsibility between shortstop and second baseman, or two outfielders, on a given play. But on offense, a man can run a play 100 times without variation or error. About the only mistake you can make is to stumble. Weighing those odds, I became extremely aggressive on the paths.

—TY COBB

OUTFIELDER, 1905–1928; LIFETIME
BATTING AVERAGE .366; LED
LEAGUE IN HITTING 12 SEASONS;
892 STOLEN BASES; MANAGER,
1921–1926; HALL OF FAME

Cheerful and popular, Rube Walker is a good receiver but his base running is a common subject of conversation.

"That guy," said a Dodger coach, "isn't as slow on the bases as he looks; he's slower."

—JAMES T. FARRELL
NOVELIST

He had larceny in his heart. But his feet were honest.

—ARTHUR "BUGS" BAER

COLUMNIST,

UPON A FAILED STEALING

ATTEMPT BY PING BODIE

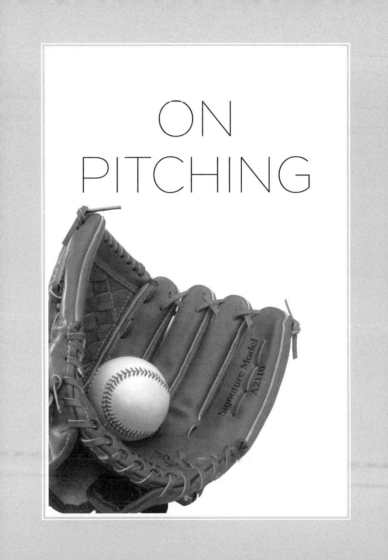

ON
PITCHING

A man should always hold something in reserve, a surprise to spring when things get tight. If a pitcher has displayed his whole assortment to the batters in the early part of the game and has used all his speed and his fastest breaking curve, then, when the crisis comes, he "hasn't anything" to fall back on.

—CHRISTY MATHEWSON
PITCHER, 1900–1916; WON 373
GAMES; MANAGER, 1916–1918;
HALL OF FAME

The real test comes when you are pitching with men on bases. Do not worry. Try to appear jolly and unconcerned. I have smiled often with the bases full with two strikes and three balls on the batter. This seems to unnerve.

—RUBE FOSTER

LONGTIME NEGRO LEAGUES PITCHER, OWNER, LEAGUE PRESIDENT; "THE FATHER OF BLACK BASEBALL"; HALL OF FAME

A curve ball may bother an ordinary hitter, but if a man is a really good hitter it's the old change of pace that causes him more trouble than all the freak deliveries in the world.

—BABE RUTH

PITCHER, OUTFIELDER. 1914–1935:
HIT 60 HOME RUNS IN 1927; 714
HOME RUNS LIFETIME; LIFETIME
.342 HITTER; COACH. 1938;
HALL OF FAME

You have to remember that every good hitter is an egotist. If you can throw the fastball past them once, they'll make any adjustment to prevent it happening again. That makes the best of them gullible for a change-up.

—WARREN SPAHN
PITCHER, 21 SEASONS, 1942–1965; WON 363 GAMES LIFETIME; HALL OF FAME

I am not positive whether a ball curves or not, but if this pitch does not curve, it would be well to notify a lot of baseball players who were forced to quit the game they love because of this pitch and may now be reached at numerous gas stations, river docks, and mental institutions.

—EDDIE SAWYER
MANAGED 1948–1952, 1958–1960;
WON ONE PENNANT

I don't know who the fellow was who came up with the first curve ball . . . I don't know when or where. But whoever he was, when he did it he took all the joy out of baseball.

—BURT SHOTTON
OUTFIELDER, 14 YEARS, 1909–1923;
MANAGER, 1927–1934, 1947–1950;
WON TWO PENNANTS; COACH

A mistake is a pitch I didn't execute well, one I left in an area where they could hit it. You don't call a ball a mistake because you miss the strike zone. That's not a mistake. A mistake, to me, is a ball I leave in the middle of the plate.

—OREL HERSHISER
PITCHER, 1983–

The knuckleball looks particularly tempting if you are a lizard or a frog.

—ROGER ANGELL

AUTHOR, EDITOR

I used to have a rifle,

I used to have a gun.

Lord, Lord,

I used to have a rifle,

I used to have a gun.

Now that ball floats over

Like a cinnamon bun.

—BLUES SONG COMPOSED BY
ROY BLOUNT, JR.
SPORTSWRITER, HUMORIST

The great [pitchers] are all competitors, they can hardly wait to get into the game. They fight you like hell when you try to take them off.

—SPARKY ANDERSON
CATCHER, 1959; MANAGER,
1970–1990; SEVEN FIRST
PLACE FINISHES, WON THREE
WORLD SERIES

The screwball. I could change speeds with it. It opened up a whole new world for me. I was like a carpenter with a whole new set of tools. It's like you have all these power tools with no electricity. Well, the screwball provided me the electricity.

—TUG McGRAW
PITCHER, 1965–1984

You do not have to be a bit touched in the head to want to earn a living as a reliever, but many relievers seem to be.

—GEORGE F. WILL
COLUMNIST

The one thing a relief pitcher hates to do is to screw up a win for a starting pitcher.

—ROLLIE FINGERS

PITCHER, 1968–1985; 341 LIFETIME SAVES; HALL OF FAME

Old timers, the generation before mine, used to say the slider was just a "nickel curve," but it wasn't that simple. It gave many pitchers a fourth pitch, and because of the fast break I found it much more difficult to pick up than the fastball, curve, or change-up.

—STAN MUSIAL
OUTFIELDER, INFIELDER, 22
SEASONS, 1941–1963; .331 LIFETIME
BATTING AVERAGE; 475 HOME
RUNS; HALL OF FAME

The better the pitcher, the earlier you have to get him. Once he gets loose and churns himself into a rhythm, hitting him will be more difficult, so you should make the most of the early opportunities. He can be like a car in the morning that won't run smoothly until it warms up.

—TIM McCARVER
CATCHER, 1959–1980;
SPORTSCASTER; SPORTSWRITER

I don't like to play cards because of the luck of the draw. But relief pitching, sure I'm in total control.

—GOOSE GOSSAGE
PITCHER, 1972–1994; 310 SAVES

Babe Ruth is Dead—throw strikes!

—ON THE T-SHIRT OF PITCHING
COACH ART FOWLER

ON
SPITBALLS

I'd go to my mouth on every pitch.
Not every pitch would be a spitball.
Sometimes I'd go maybe two or three
innings without throwing one. But
I'd always have them looking for it.

—STANLEY COVALESKI
PITCHER, 16 SEASONS,
1912–1928; WON 215 GAMES;
HALL OF FAME

I used to chew slippery elm—the bark, right off the tree. Come spring the bark would get nice and loose and you could slice it free without any trouble. What I chewed was the fiber from inside, and that's what I put on the ball. That's what they called the foreign substance. The ball would break like hell, away from right-handed hitters, and in on lefties.

—BURLEIGH GRIMES
PITCHER, 1916–1934; 270 LIFETIME
WINS; MANAGER, 1937–1938;
HALL OF FAME

I sometimes missed that sinker of [Johnny Allen's] day by a foot. It wasn't a curve and it wasn't a fastball, so I took it for granted it was a slider. But come to think of it, I did not in those days miss sliders by a foot.

—JOE DIMAGGIO
OUTFIELDER, 13 SEASONS,
1936–1948; .325 LIFETIME HITTER;
HIT IN 56 CONSECUTIVE GAMES,
1941; HALL OF FAME

The batter's sitting in the circle with a pine tar cloth. Puts tar on his hands, up to his elbows, if he wants, and rubs that bat and gets up there and squeezes and it sounds like a dad-gum car comin' by you, screechin' its wheels.

But if it's a poor old pitcher, he better not put his hand in his pocket, or touch his hat ever, 'cause they're gonna come runnin' to shake him down. I don't get it.

—PREACHER ROE
PITCHER, 1938, 1944–1954

Give the pitchers the right to apply saliva to the ball and you might give them the impression that they would be winked at if they again laved the ball with tobacco juice, annointed it with oils, powdered it with talcum, or even stuck phono-graph needles in it.

—BRANCH RICKEY
CATCHER, 1905–1907, 1914;
MANAGER, TEN SEASONS, 1913–1925;
EXECUTIVE, 1910s–1950s;
PIONEERED IN FARM SYSTEM;
ENDED RACIAL SEGREGATION
IN PROFESSIONAL BASEBALL;
HALL OF FAME

Let them revive the spitter and help the pitchers make a living.

—CASEY STENGEL
OUTFIELDER, 1912–1925; MANAGER,
1934–1943, 1949–1960, 1962–1965;
WON TEN PENNANTS, SEVEN
WORLD SERIES, FIVE IN A ROW;
COACH; HALL OF FAME

I see no need to revive it. All of us in baseball know that it's being thrown occasionally anyway.

—WALTER ALSTON

PITCHER, 1936; MANAGER 1954–1976; FINISHED FIRST SEVEN TIMES, WON FOUR WORLD SERIES; HALL OF FAME

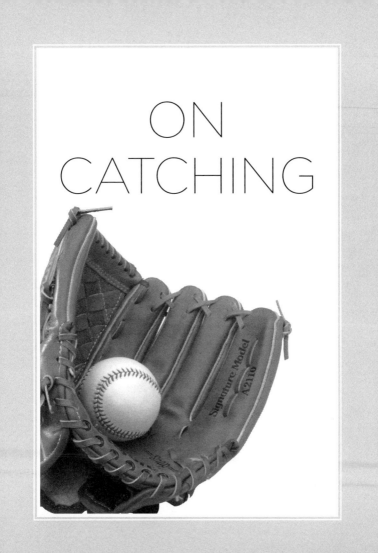

ON
CATCHING

I think we should look at the other end of the battery and consider the possibility that, year in and year out, each of the well-established veteran catchers is almost surely the most valuable player on his club . . .

—ROGER ANGELL
AUTHOR, EDITOR

A catcher and his body are like the outlaw and his horse. He's got to ride that nag till it drops.

—JOHNNY BENCH
CATCHER, 1967–1983; 385 HOME RUNS; HALL OF FAME

Masochists are what they are. A man has to love to get banged up if he deliberately chooses to be a catcher.

—JIM BROSNAN
PITCHER, NINE SEASONS. 1954–1963;
AUTHOR; SPORTSCASTER

What I've seen over the past fifteen to twenty years is that the quickest route to the major leagues is by being a catcher.

—RAY HAYWORTH
CATCHER, 15 SEASONS, 1926–1945

When I was making the transition from shortstop to catcher, one of the things they used to teach in that situation was to look the runner back to third before you threw to second. Well, if I've looked down there a thousand times, I still haven't seen anything. I look, all right, but as far as seeing if he's got a twenty-foot lead or a ten-foot lead or if he's standing on the bag, I would never see it because if you look long enough to actually see what's there, there's no way you're going to throw the man out at second.

—BOBBY BRAGAN
   CATCHER, SIX SEASONS, 1941–1948;
   MANAGER, 1956–1958, 1963–1966;
   COACH

I got one that can throw, but can't catch, and one that can catch but can't throw. And one who can hit but can't do either.

—CASEY STENGEL

OUTFIELDER, 1912–1925; MANAGER, 1934–1943, 1949–1960, 1962–1965; WON TEN PENNANTS, SEVEN WORLD SERIES, FIVE IN A ROW; COACH; HALL OF FAME

Anyway, who knows what the right pitch should have been? Most of the time you do everything right and a Mark McGwire, Tino Martinez or Barry Bonds will still pop it.

—TIM McCARVER
CATCHER, 1959–1980;
SPORTSCASTER; SPORTSWRITER

ON
DEFENSE

Championship baseball teams are not founded on bats. They're built on a backbone of catching, pitching, a second-base combination and a center fielder.

—CARL MAYS
PITCHER, 1915–1929;
208 LIFETIME WINS

Now that I think of it, some of the best preparation for outfield might be playing infield.

—DICK HOWSER

INFIELDER. 1961-68; MANAGER, 1980-1986; THREE FIRST PLACE FINISHES. WON ONE WORLD SERIES; COACH

The third base is not quite as important a position as the others, but it nevertheless requires its occupant to be a good player, as some very pretty play is frequently shown on this base.

—SEYMOUR R. CHURCH

SPORTSWRITER, LATE 19TH TO EARLY 20TH CENTURY

The shortstop—I don't know what's the hardest play for him. They're all hard, I guess. There's not much of a problem for him on the double play, because the whole situation's right in front of him, but the second baseman—he knows he's got to turn that thing, and the guy's breathing down his neck. You can get your legs torn up. More often than not, you see the second baseman turn it when he doesn't have a chance, really. The judgment of infielders is something.

—CLETE BOYER
INFIELDER, 1955–1971

You don't see too many big-legged second basemen, or big-legged shortstops. Why? Any scout could tell you. Range! The ones with range have tiny little legs.

—GEORGE KISSELL

COACH, 1969–1975; SCOUT

On September 13, 1942, Cub shortstop Len Merullo booted four plays in one inning. That morning his wife had given birth to a son. A sportswriter named the boy Boots Merullo.

—JIM KAPLAN
SPORTSWRITER, AUTHOR

The thing about the pickoff play is not just the twenty-six or twenty-seven guys you get a year—and I don't want to minimize that—but it just kills a ballclub. It happens to us every once in a while, and you can just feel the whole club go flat.

—RAY MILLER

MANAGER, 1985–1986, 1999; COACH

Take Larry Bowa and Garry Templeton in 1978. That year Bowa won his last Gold Glove, making only ten errors and leading the league in fielding percentage at .986. Templeton was an erratic twenty-two-year-old shortstop who led the league in errors and fielded only .953. What do we learn from this thirty-three-point difference? Did we learn that Templeton—years away from his later knee trouble—showed spectacular range and fielded 82 more balls cleanly than Bowa did, despite playing one fewer game? Did we learn that Templeton led the league's shortstops in double plays with 108 compared with Bowa's 80?

—CRAIG R. WRIGHT
SPORTSWRITER,
BASEBALL STATISTICIAN

[Bill Terry] concentrated entirely on defense. His theory was not to let the other club score and they'd beat themselves. Naturally most ball games are lost rather than won. Terry took it far beyond anything I ever knew—his entire approach in every game was defense. He didn't hit-and-run. He didn't go for the stolen base or any offensive plays at all. He just figured to score three or four runs.

—PAUL RICHARDS
CATCHER, 1932–1935, 1942–1946;
MANAGER, 1952–1961, 1976

[Casey Stengel] relished double plays and was always looking for deft second basemen who could "make the pivot." He called the double play the most important play in baseball. "It's two-thirds of an inning!" he'd say. "One ground ball and [slap of the hands] two! You're out of the inning."

—ROBERT W. CREAMER
**SPORTSWRITER,
BIOGRAPHER, EDITOR**

ON
RETIREMENT

Having to leave the game is a very difficult adjustment to make, and that goes for every single ballplayer. Don't let any one of them tell you different.

—BILL WAMBSGANSS
INFIELDER, 1914–1926

I don't miss the pitching but I can't say I don't miss the game. I miss it a little. There's a lot I don't want to get back to. . . . I think it's the life I miss—all the activities that's around baseball. I don't miss playing baseball but I miss . . . baseball. Baseball. Does that sound like a crazy man?

—BOB GIBSON
PITCHER, 1959–1975; 251 GAMES WON; COACH; HALL OF FAME

. . . my years in baseball had their ups and downs, their strife and their torment. But the years I look at most fondly, and those I'd most like to live over, are the years when I was playing center field for the New York Giants.

—FRED SNODGRASS
OUTFIELDER, 1908–1916

Of course, finally, after about 20 years, I figured I'd had it. Forty years old, it gets to be a little too much like work. The old bones stiffen up and get a little frickle, you know, and then it's about time to stop. Anyway, you can't live out of a grip forever . . . hotel . . . taxi . . . train . . . taxi . . . hotel . . . train . . . and then all over again.

—GOOSE GOSLIN
**OUTFIELDER, 1921–1938; .316
LIFETIME BATTING AVERAGE;
HALL OF FAME**

There's always the temptation to try that one more year, to see if you can wind up the clock again. But you find out soon enough that it's a game where youth dominates. You remember when you came up yourself, full of springtime, and pushed somebody else aside. So you have to be philosophical about it. You'd better be.

—TED KLUSZEWSKI
INFIELDER, 1947–1961

For a while after you leave
the game, you dream about
it a lot. You dream that you're
going to pitch and can't get
your uniform on. You dream
that you can't get to the park,
that you've lost your way.

—WES FERRELL
PITCHER, 1927–1941

The main difference between being a player and a broadcaster is I don't have to keep in shape.

—RALPH KINER

OUTFIELDER, 1946–1955; 369 LIFETIME HOME RUNS; SPORTSCASTER; HALL OF FAME

You see, you spend a good piece of your life gripping a baseball; and in the end it turns out that it was the other way around all the time.

—JIM BOUTON
PITCHER, 1962–1970, 1978; AUTHOR

ON
MANAGERS

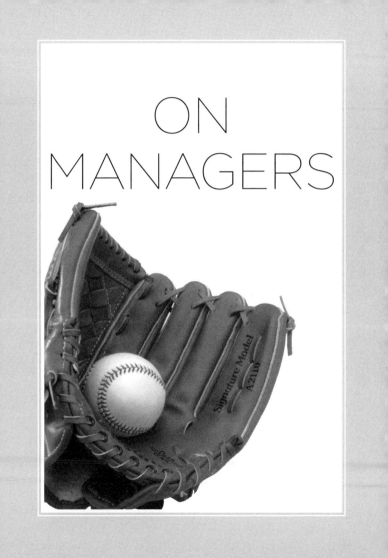

"Don't give him anything good, but don't walk him."

—ROGERS HORNSBY
INFIELDER, 1915–1937; .358 LIFETIME
BATTING AVERAGE; MANAGER,
14 SEASONS, 1925–1937, 1952–1953;
HALL OF FAME,
TO BURLEIGH GRIMES

There are three things the average man thinks he can do better than anyone else: build a fire, run a hotel and manage a baseball team.

—ROCKY BRIDGES
INFIELDER, 1951-1961; COACH

Billy, what I can't understand is how I got so smart so fast, and you got so dumb.

—CASEY STENGEL
OUTFIELDER, 1912–1925; MANAGER, 1934–1943, 1949–1960, 1962–1965; WON TEN PENNANTS, SEVEN WORLD SERIES, FIVE IN A ROW; COACH; HALL OF FAME, TO PITTSBURGH MANAGER BILLY MEYER AFTER THE PIRATES FELL TO EIGHTH PLACE IN 1950 WHILE STENGEL'S YANKEES WON THE PENNANT AND WORLD SERIES

One day when I visited the Yankees bench I commented on the number of players Stengel was using nearly every day. Casey pointed to the row of pinstriped players who rode the bench with him. "None of those guys board here; they all work. That's why they give us twenty-five players—to let the manager play games with them."

—FRED LIEB
SPORTSWRITER

Today big-league managers come and go.
Charlie Finley hired and fired them, then George
Steinbrenner outdid Finley. Led by Finley and
followed by Steinbrenner, major-league owners
have debased the lofty status of manager and
stripped that position of much of the honor it
once commanded.

—RED BARBER
SPORTSCASTER, AUTHOR

I have never believed it effective to use ace against ace. From the grandstand and crowd point of view, this is all right, but when it comes to winning games throughout the season the percentage is against it. Why sacrifice an almost certain win for a possible low-score loss?

—MICKEY COCHRANE
CATCHER, 1925–1937; .320 LIFETIME
BATTING AVERAGE; MANAGER,
1934–1938; WON TWO PENNANTS,
ONE WORLD SERIES;
HALL OF FAME

The crowd which cheers the players has little conception of the trials and tribulations of the manager who crouches unseen and forgotten . . . in the corner of the bench. The public does not realize that he is dealing with twenty-two ultra-independent athletes, vulgarly healthy, frankly outspoken, and unawed by any authority or pomp. Only persons who have one child, which possesses four grandparents, and twenty or thirty aunts all trying to spoil it, can understand in full the difficulties of the manager's job.

—JOHNNY EVERS
INFIELDER, 1902–1917; "TINKER TO EVANS TO CHANCE"; MANAGER, 1913, 1921, 1924; HALL OF FAME

I had another system I used now and then when I wanted to know who was staying out late. It was very simple. I gave the night elevator operator a brand new baseball and told him to get the players to autograph it for him. So as they came in at night, they'd sign the ball. The next day he'd show me the ball and tell me what time each man came in.

—EDDIE SAWYER
**MANAGED 1948–1952, 1958–1960;
WON ONE PENNANT**

All Earl [Weaver] under-
stood about the curve-
ball is that he couldn't
hit one. So that's what
he wanted you to throw.

—JIM PALMER

PITCHER, 19 SEASONS, 1965–1984;

268 LIFETIME WINS; HALL OF FAME

When [Gil] Hodges managed the Washington Senators, he learned once that four players were violating a midnight curfew. Hodges believes in curfews and he summoned his ball club and announced: "I know who you were. You're each fined one hundred dollars. But a lot of us are married and I don't want to embarrass anyone. There's a cigar box on my desk. At the end of the day I'm going to look into that box and I want to see four hundred dollars in it. Then the matter will be closed." Hodges gazed. At the end of the day, he looked into the cigar box. He found $700.

—ROGER KAHN
SPORTSWRITER

While managing the Cubs, Don Zimmer once had a player come in to complain about not being in the lineup. Zimmer had the player change places with him and sit behind the manager's desk. And Zimmer took the role of the player and said, "How can you not start me although the two guys ahead of me are playing better?" Then Zimmer asked the player to respond as if he were Don Zimmer. The guy walked out with no argument.

—TIM McCARVER
CATCHER, 1959–1980;
SPORTSCASTER; SPORTSWRITER

Well, you can just do it somewhere else.
I'm sick and tired of this bullshit. I've
been kissing your ass for five years and
I'm sick and fucking tired of it, do you
hear me? If you don't like the way you're
treated here or you don't like our rules,
then take off the goddamn uniform and
get the hell out of here because you're
not going to turn this team upside down.
If you don't like it here, then get the
fuck out of here.

—JIM LEYLAND
MANAGER, 1986–1999; COACH,
AFTER BARRY BONDS HAD
THROWN A TEMPER TANTRUM
AT A PHOTOGRAPHER

If you have some good horses you can win the race, but you can't win anything with a bunch of mules.

—EDDIE MOORE

INFIELDER, OUTFIELDER, TEN SEASONS, 1923–1934

You know me. I don't get
no kick out of a humpty
dumpty club.

—ROGERS HORNSBY
INFIELDER, 1915–1937; .358 LIFETIME
BATTING AVERAGE; MANAGER,
14 SEASONS. 1925–1937. 1952–1953;
HALL OF FAME

Just stay away from firearms,
Red, and don't room higher
than the second floor. You
might want to jump.

—FRANK FRISCH
INFIELDER, 1919-1937; LIFETIME
.316 HITTER; MANAGER, 16 YEARS,
1933-1951; HALL OF FAME,
GIVING ADVICE TO THE NEW
MANAGER OF THE ST. LOUIS
CARDINALS, RED SCHOENDIENST

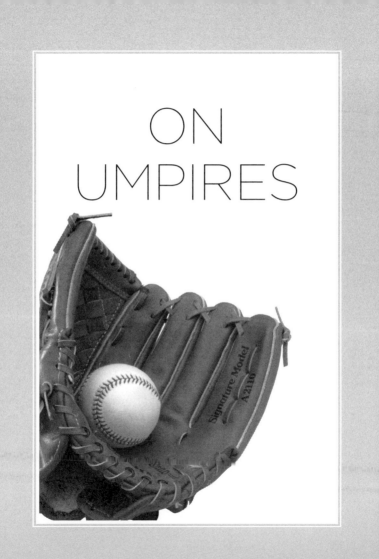

ON
UMPIRES

Outside of the nine players on each side there is another important personage, known as "The Umpire." He is not placed there as a target for the malediction of disappointed spectators. He is of flesh and blood, and has feelings just the same as any other human being.

—JOHN MONTGOMERY WARD
PITCHER, INFIELDER, OUTFIELDER, 1878–1894; MANAGER, SEVEN SEASONS, 1880–1894; OWNER, 1912; HALL OF FAME

One thing there is that affords a baseball umpire consolation, and that is the thought that he can die only once, and then never more.

—*THE SPORTING NEWS*, 1888

There are no close plays. A man is always out or safe, or it is a ball or a strike, and the umpire, if he is a good man and knows his business, is always right. For instance, I am always right.

—SILK O'LOUGHLIN

UMPIRE, 1902–1918

When Lord Bill [Byron] called what McGraw thought was a bad one, Mac would start for the umpire, and Byron would begin to sing, "Here Comes McGraw" to the tune of Mendelssohn's "Wedding March."*

—JOE WILLIAMS
COLUMNIST, 1910s–1950s

[*—Actually the "Bridal Chorus" from Wagner's *Lohengrin*. –ed.]

Johnson was working against us and they was two out and Collins on second base and Silk [O'Loughlin] called a third strike on Gandil that was down by his corns. So Gleason hollered "All right Silk you won't have to go to war. You couldn't pass the eye test." So Silk told him to get off the field. So then I hollered something at Silk and he hollered back at me "That will be all from you you big busher." So I said "You are a busher yourself you busher." So he said:

"Get off the bench and let one of the ball players sit down."

—RING LARDNER
SPORTSWRITER, AUTHOR,
HUMORIST

February 22, 1889. — Umpire Magill, with a bat, fractured the skull of a spectator who took exception to his rulings in an exhibition game. Chattanooga.

—SEYMOUR R. CHURCH

SPORTSWRITER, LATE 19TH TO EARLY 20TH CENTURY

If dat bat comes down,
you're outta da game.

—BILL GUTHRIE

UMPIRE, NINE SEASONS, 1913–1932,
AFTER A BATTER HEAVED HIS BAT
SKYWARD UPON BEING CALLED
OUT ON STRIKES

The greatest umpire who ever lived was Bill Klem. He summed up his profession in one terse sentence: "Umpire the ball."

—RED BARBER
SPORTSCASTER, AUTHOR

I was fired out of so many games on my ear last summer by these human walruses in umpire suits that I think my ears must have callouses on them. And instead of sympathizing with me, everybody seemed to sympathize with the umpires.

—JOHNNY EVERS

INFIELDER, 1902–1917; "TINKER TO EVANS TO CHANCE"; MANAGER, 1913, 1921, 1924; HALL OF FAME

While we were playing at Philadelphia, Charles Pfirman, the umpire, and Manager Art Fletcher got into a real fight. Pfirman hit Fletcher over the head with his mask, which brought the fight to an end. When the fight started, Bob Hart, the first base umpire, ran to Pfirman's aid. He was right in the middle of the fight and got a real pushing around.

After the fight was over I went over to Bob Hart and said, "Bob, your face is all scratched up. Wait a minute and I'll get some Mercurochrome for you." (Bob didn't have a scratch on him.) I yelled into the bench and said, "Hey, bring out that Mercurochrome." I painted Bob's face until he looked like a zebra. The next day when Bob came on the field he came over to me, and what he called me I dare not print.

—RABBIT MARANVILLE
INFIELDER, 1912–1935;
HALL OF FAME

When Chub Feeney became president of the National League in 1970, he required all umpires on opening day "to shake hands with each manager and wish him luck." [Tom] Gorman was umpiring a game that involved a Durocher team, and he called Feeney to refuse the charge; Feeney said that noncompliance would cost him three hundred dollars. Gorman breathed deeply, and at the appointed hour approached Durocher.

"Hello, Leo, it's nice to see you. The best of luck for the rest of the season."

Durocher was adequate to the occasion. "Horseshit," he said.

—DONALD HALL
POET, BASEBALL HISTORIAN

Finally [George Magerkurth] wheeled on me and yelled, "That's all, you're out of the park." And when he said "park," the tobacco juice splattered me across the face like a summer monsoon. So I took a leap at him and I spit right in his face. . . .

"That'll cost you two hundred fifty dollars and ten days," Magerkurth roared.

"For what?"

"You spat in my face."

"What the hell do you think this is?" I said, pointing. "Smallpox?"

—LEO DUROCHER
INFIELDER, 17 YEARS, 1925–1945;
MANAGER, 24 YEARS, 1939–1973;
WON THREE PENNANTS, ONE
WORLD SERIES; HALL OF FAME

Another of the better umpires [in the Negro leagues] was John Craig, from Pittsburgh. There were some other good umps from around that area but if you ever got out there, they would always favor the Homestead Grays. If a critical play came up you could almost bet that the Grays would get the benefit of the call. . . . One time Craig and the other umpires came out on the field before a game and little Jimmy Hill said, "Well, here comes Jesse James and the Dalton boys." The umpires wanted to eject him before the game started but the league officials in attendance wouldn't let them.

—MONTE IRVIN
STAR IN NEGRO LEAGUES;
INFIELDER, OUTFIELDER, 1949–1956;
HALL OF FAME

[Bill] Haller and [Earl] Weaver had had difficulties for a long time. One Saturday afternoon Haller was working the plate and looked over at the Oriole dugout and spotted Weaver on his knees on the steps. Bill wandered over there and quietly asked him to leave the premises without hesitation. Weaver couldn't believe it. "What're you throwing me out for?" he demanded. "I'm just praying. You can't throw me out for praying."

"You Jewish?"

"No," Weaver admitted.

Haller smiled. "Well, it's Saturday, and you don't pray on Saturday if you're not Jewish. So get outta here."

—RON LUCIANO
UMPIRE, 1968-1980; AUTHOR

I represent the integrity of the game and I'm going to do it if necessary.

—DOUG HARVEY

UMPIRE, 1962–1993,
UPON EJECTING DON SUTTON
FROM A GAME AFTER COLLECTING
THREE BASEBALLS THAT WERE
SCUFFED

Players and managers respect confidence; they want to see it. The other night one of them hollered out to me, "That was a balk." I looked at him and said, "I wrote the book on balks." They laughed, and then one of them said, "I bet it wasn't very thick."

—DURWOOD MERRILL
UMPIRE, 1977–

I worked with an ump
in the Northern League
and I was the only one
who knew that he had
a glass eye.

—KEN KAISER

UMPIRE, 1977–

ON
SCOUTING

Scouts are still probably the lowest
paid employees in the baseball chain.

—MAURY ALLEN
BASEBALL HISTORIAN

. . . the writer, Harold Parrott, told an interesting one about "Vinegar Bill" Essick, the Yankee scout who signed Joe Gordon. He was trying to sign a young prospect named Johnny Lindell. The night he called on Lindell's parents, Essick played a few selections from Brahms. And the parents hearing the scout at the piano, decided that after all, baseball couldn't be so rowdy. Johnny Lindell was signed, and his batting helped the New York Yankees to win a World Series.

—JAMES T. FARRELL
NOVELIST

The draft is socialistic. For one thing, it gives the teams with the poorest records the earliest selections in each round. It's part of a push to equalize talent from team to team—but there never has been equalization of talent in baseball, and there never will be.

—PAUL OWENS
SCOUT

If scouting were just a matter of signing the guys who hit the home runs and pitch the no-hitters, anybody could do it. But the major league prospect might be the guy who has something special even though he struck out swinging or overthrew the third baseman from right field or walked nine batters. Tools we call them: speed, arm strength, range, hands, bat speed.

—BUCK O'NEIL
STAR PLAYER, MANAGER IN NEGRO LEAGUES; COACH; SCOUT

Looks like Tarzan.
Runs like Jane.

—SCOUTING REPORT

ON THE
NEGRO
LEAGUES

Yet when you look back, what people
didn't realize, and still don't, was that
we got the ball rolling on integration
in our whole society. Remember, this
was before Brown versus the Board
of Education of Topeka. When Branch
Rickey signed Jackie, Martin Luther
King was a student at Morris College.
We showed the way it had to be done,
by just keeping on and being the best
we could.

—BUCK O'NEIL
**STAR PLAYER, MANAGER IN NEGRO
LEAGUES; COACH; SCOUT**

We suggest that every citation for a record set before 1950 should bear an asterisk, with the following explanation:

* Set before the American and National Leagues became the major leagues.

—JOHN B. HOLWAY
BASEBALL HISTORIAN

If you want to know the truth, Judy, there are just too many of you to go in.

—CONNIE MACK

CATCHER, 1886–1896; MANAGER, 53 SEASONS, 1894–1950; WON EIGHT PENNANTS, FIVE WORLD SERIES; HALL OF FAME, WHEN ASKED BY JUDY JOHNSON WHY AS A STAR BLACK PLAYER HE DID NOT MAKE THE MAJOR LEAGUES

I made more money when I was in the majors, and the caliber of baseball and the playing conditions were better, but I had more fun with the Negro leagues.

—MONTE IRVIN
  STAR IN NEGRO LEAGUES;
  INFIELDER, OUTFIELDER, 1949–1956;
  HALL OF FAME

Whether we get any recognition for it may be considered beside the point. We want Jackie [Robinson] to have a chance.

—J. L. WILKINSON

OWNER, KANSAS CITY MONARCHS

The Brooklyn Dodgers today purchased the contract of Jackie Roosevelt Robinson from the Montreal Royals. He will report immediately.

—BRANCH RICKEY
CATCHER, 1905–1907, 1914;
MANAGER, TEN SEASONS,
1913–1925; EXECUTIVE, 1910s–1950s;
PIONEERED IN FARM SYSTEM;
ENDED RACIAL SEGREGATION
IN PROFESSIONAL BASEBALL;
HALL OF FAME,
NEWS RELEASE ISSUED APRIL
10, 1947

When [Hank] Thompson and I reported to the
Polo Grounds, our uniforms were laid out for us.
I went over to the locker to get dressed, and when
I put on the New York Giants uniform for the first
time, that had to be one of the greatest thrills
of my life. It was like a dream coming true, and
something that I never expected to ever happen.
I thought about the long road that I had traveled
to get there, and the fact that it was finally happening was a feeling that is indescribable.

—MONTE IRVIN
STAR IN NEGRO LEAGUES;
INFIELDER, OUTFIELDER, 1949-1956;
HALL OF FAME

When Jackie Robinson died in 1972 of diabetes and hypertension, some wrote that his coming was no big thing and would have happened sooner or later. Others, more cynical, described Rickey's driving force as greed. But the fact is that before Branch Rickey no one had done it or even seriously proposed doing it. And that is his legacy.

—MURRAY POLNER
AUTHOR, BIOGRAPHER

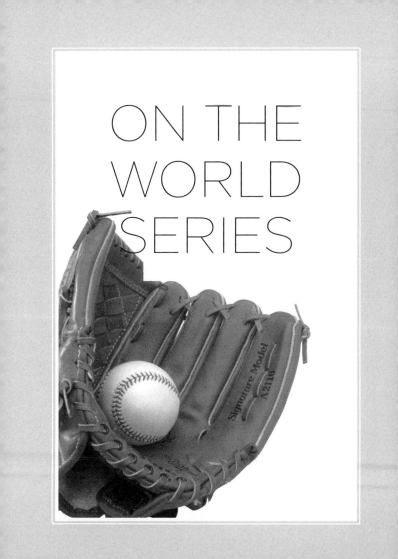

ON THE
WORLD
SERIES

Casey [Stengel] always had something to say, even in those days. I remember, just before the first game (of the 1916 Series), during batting practice, Duffy Lewis and I were walking across the outfield and as we passed him Casey said, "Hello, boys. What do you think your losing share is going to come to?"

—ERNIE SHORE
PITCHER, SEVEN YEARS, 1912–1920

It's like the Fourth of July, New Year's Eve, and your birthday all wrapped in one.

—TOM SEAVER

PITCHER, 1967–1986; 311 LIFETIME
VICTORIES; HALL OF FAME

It doesn't get any better than winning the World Series.

—CHUCK KNOBLAUCH

INFIELDER, 1991–

ON
FANS

The feebleness of the home team's play . . . caused much dissatisfaction, which was rather warmly expressed.

—*BALTIMORE SUN*, 1874

The voice of the republic is not a pontifical blessing from a high window or the cry of an imperial herald in a palace court. It is the voice of a crowd, best heard in its spontaneity in a ball park.

—MARSHALL SMELSER

BASEBALL HISTORIAN, BIOGRAPHER, UNIVERSITY PROFESSOR

The lesser wonders of baseball—the sacrifice fly, the three-six-three double play, the wrong-side hit-and-run bouncer through a vacated infield sector, the right-field-to-third-base peg that cuts down a lead runner, the extended turn at bat against an obdurate pitcher that ends with a crucial single squiggled down the middle—are most appreciated by the experienced fan, who may in time also come to understand that expertise is the best defense against partisanship.

—ROGER ANGELL
AUTHOR, EDITOR

It has been decided that the American baseball fan should have a distinctive dress. A choice has been made from among the more popular styles and the following has been designated as regulation, embodying, as it does, the spirit and tone of the great national pastime.

Straw hat, worn well back on the head; one cigar, unlighted, held between teeth; vest worn but unbuttoned and open, displaying both a belt and suspenders, with gold watchchain connecting the bottom pockets.

—ROBERT BENCHLEY
HUMORIST. 1920s–1940s

There are more good batters and umpires and all-round ball players in the grand stand within one's hearing, than are to be found in both the contesting teams.

—JOHN MONTGOMERY WARD
PITCHER, INFIELDER, OUTFIELDER, 1878–1894; MANAGER, SEVEN SEASONS, 1880–1894; OWNER, 1912; HALL OF FAME

A people who can become as excited about anything as the majority of New Yorkers can about the baseball pennant is far from being lost to hope.

—*NEW YORK AMERICAN*, OCT. 9, 1908

Well, throwing things
on the field is not my
idea of a well-rounded
human being.

—STEVE GARVEY

INFIELDER, 1969–1987,
WHEN ASKED BY A REPORTER
WHAT HE THOUGHT OF THE
FANS AT YANKEE STADIUM.

This year, after a game with the Orioles—which the Yankees won—I waited outside the players' gate with Elrod Hendricks, the Orioles' coach who once played for the Yankees. A howling mob stood behind police barricades, jeering and screaming obscenities at each of the Oriole players who boarded a waiting team bus. This was standard, Hendricks assured me—for Yankee Stadium.

—DAVID FALKNER
AUTHOR, ACTOR

Over in Brooklyn they don't bet that the home team will win—they make book on how much the opposing forces will win by. This sport furnishes the only uncertainty of the entertainment.

—W. H. AULICK
NEWSPAPER SPORTSWRITER,
NEW YORK TIMES, MAY 31, 1908

The bottle has a peculiar significance in Brooklyn. Were there a baseball crest for the Dodgers it would show a pop bottle rampant on a field strewn with umpires.

—JOE WILLIAMS
COLUMNIST, 1910s-1950s

Jeez! It's Poil Harbor for da Giants.

—BROOKLYN DODGER FAN
QUOTED AFTER LEO DUROCHER
WAS APPOINTED MANAGER OF
THE NEW YORK GIANTS,
REPLACING MEL OTT

If I close my eyes against the sun [at Fenway Park], all at once I am back at Ebbets Field, a young girl once more in the presence of my father, watching the players of my youth on the grassy field below. There is magic in this moment, for when I open my eyes and see my sons in the place where my father once sat, I feel an invisible bond between our three generations, an anchor of loyalty linking my sons to the grandfather whose face they never saw but whose person they have already come to know through the most timeless of all sports, the game of baseball.

—DORIS KEARNS GOODWIN
HISTORIAN, UNIVERSITY
PROFESSOR, AUTHOR

I enjoy Shea Stadium. But the fans are something else. I look upon each game there as an experience. I get to go to a zoo and don't have to pay admission.

—PETE ROSE

INFIELDER, OUTFIELDER, 1963–1986; SET LIFETIME RECORDS OF 3,562 MAJOR LEAGUE GAMES PLAYED, 14,053 TIMES AT BAT, 4,256 BASE HITS; MANAGER, 1984–1986; BANNED FROM BASEBALL IN 1989 FOR GAMBLING

There aren't many people coming to see us play these days, and those two pay a dollar and a half each to come in. They can holler anything they like.

—CONNIE MACK

CATCHER, 1886–1896; MANAGER, 53 SEASONS, 1894–1950; WON EIGHT PENNANTS, FIVE WORLD SERIES; HALL OF FAME,

REFUSING HIS PLAYERS' REQUEST TO HAVE TWO LOUD, ABUSIVE FANS EJECTED FROM SHIBE PARK

When Lou Piniella used to play the outfield for the Royals and Yankees, he'd yell at hecklers in the stands, "Go home and check your wife, we've got a ballplayer missing."

—TIM McCARVER
CATCHER, 1959–1980;
SPORTSCASTER; SPORTSWRITER

Baseball fans have short memories. I've even seen them boo Walter Johnson, and in my opinion he was the greatest pitcher who ever lived.

—SPECTATOR AT MEMORIAL STADIUM, BALTIMORE, 1952.

Most of the White Sox fans cheer for the Cubs when the Cubs are in first place, but Cub fans never, never cheer for the White Sox. They sort of don't notice them.

—TIM SHANAHAN
UNIVERSITY PROFESSOR

[Casey Stengel] was amused by the fans. He used to talk later about the ones who sat on fire escapes on buildings beyond the outfield fence and watched the games from there. It cost them only ten cents for a pail of beer to sit up there, and, Casey said, "They didn't get real insulting until the beer began to take effect about the fourth inning."

—ROBERT W. CREAMER
SPORTSWRITER, BIOGRAPHER, EDITOR

To bolster attendance, the Cleveland Indians designated their June 4, 1974, contest with the Texas Rangers a special "10-cent Beer Night" and lived to regret it. With the score tied 5–5 in the bottom of the ninth and the winning Cleveland run perched on third base with two out, Tribe fans in various stages of inebriation poured out of the rightfield stands and began tussling with Texas outfielder Jeff Burroughs. When Burroughs fought back benches emptied to protect him. Order was eventually restored, but the peace was short-lived. After umpire Nestor Chylak was struck on the head in a fresh melee, the game was forfeited to Texas.

—DAVID NEMEC
BASEBALL HISTORIAN

This man was on his feet at Veterans Stadium, along with a friend and 65,836 other disbelieving partisans, as the sixth game ran down to its last out, and was startled to discover that he felt exactly like the victorious but expiring Lord Nelson at the Battle of Trafalgar. Tug McGraw wound and threw, Willie Wilson swung and missed, and as the last great roar of pleasure split the night sky and the green Astro Turf below was suddenly emptied of baseball and filled, weirdly, with police horses and police attack dogs, my friend, tottering, leaned toward his companion and croaked, "Kiss me, Hardy."

—ROGER ANGELL
AUTHOR, EDITOR

The real article is the man who knows most of the players by sight, as they appear on the field, but wouldn't know more than one or two of them if he saw them on the street, struggles hard to keep an accurate score and makes a mistake on every other play, or doesn't attempt to score at all, disputes every statement made by his neighbors in the bleachers whether he knows anything about said statement or not, heaps imprecations on the umpire and the manager, thinks something is a bonehead play when it really is good, clever baseball, talks fluently about Mathewson's "inshoot," believes that Hank O'Day has it in for the home team and is purposely making bad decisions, and says "Bransfield is going to bat for Moore" when Walsh is sent in to hit for Chalmers.

—RING LARDNER
SPORTSWRITER, AUTHOR,
HUMORIST

On the way out, in the eighth inning, I saw a young groupie approach George Foster just outside the Cincinnati clubhouse. "Sign my pants!" she said to him. "Please, George, sign my pants!"

We both looked, and, sure enough, her bluejeans were heavily autographed.

"I don't sign clothing," Foster said.

—ROGER ANGELL
AUTHOR, EDITOR

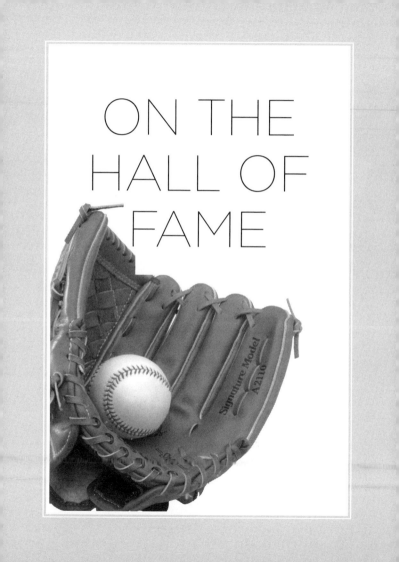

ON THE
HALL OF
FAME

Records, yes I've got a few of those too, but records are made to be broken. If you've got one that stands up, well you know that somebody might come along and break it. And then they might not, that's what baseball records are all about. But the Hall of Fame, that will be there forever.

—HOYT WILHELM
PITCHER, 1952–1972; WON 123 GAMES IN RELIEF; HALL OF FAME

You look at the lineup we put on the field for the first game of that [1932] World Series and you'll see we had six fellows in there who are in the Hall of Fame today—Ruth, Gehrig, Combs, Dickey, Red Ruffing, and myself.

—JOE SEWELL
INFIELDER, 1920–1933; LIFETIME .312
HITTER; HALL OF FAME

I know it's hard to get into the Hall of Fame. I don't know what kept me out—maybe it was the writers—but I finally made it and I thank God for it. I didn't know I'd ever feel like this.

—BILL TERRY

INFIELDER, 1923–1936;
LIFETIME .341 BATTING AVERAGE;
MANAGER, 1932–1941; WON THREE
PENNANTS, ONE WORLD SERIES;
HALL OF FAME

He came in the front door [of the Hall of Fame], but the original plan was for him to go in the back door: into a special wing for Negro-leaguers. A lot of people, black and white, were angry when that plan was announced, and I think Satchel shook them up when he said, "The only change is that baseball has turned Satchel from a second-class citizen into a second-class immortal." The outcry was such that Commissioner Bowie Kuhn reversed the decision and put Satchel in the same room with Ruth and Mathewson and Jackie Robinson.

—BUCK O'NEIL
STAR PLAYER, MANAGER IN NEGRO
LEAGUES; COACH; SCOUT

We never thought we'd get in the Hall of Fame. It was so far from us, we didn't even consider it. We didn't even think it would some day come to reality. We thought the way we were playing was the way it was going to continue. I never had any dream it would come. But last night I felt like I was part of it at last.

—BUCK LEONARD
STAR INFIELDER IN NEGRO
LEAGUES, 1933–1950: HALL OF FAME

ON
INNOVATION

In the country of baseball days

are always the same.

—DONALD HALL

POET, BASEBALL HISTORIAN

Baseball's essential rules for place and for play were established, to my reckoning, with almost no exceptions of consequence, by 1895.

—A. BARTLETT GIAMATTI
UNIVERSITY PROFESSOR, PRESIDENT; PRESIDENT, NATIONAL LEAGUE, 1986–1989; COMMISSIONER OF BASEBALL, 1989–1992

The coincidence . . . of electronic public-address systems and World War II brought about the current practice of playing the anthem before every baseball game (and, by extension, before practically every major sports event). It is estimated that a twenty-year veteran like Willie Mays heard "The Star-Spangled Banner" played 3000 times. Usually badly.

—ROBERT W. CREAMER
SPORTSWRITER, BIOGRAPHER,
EDITOR

It is the same game that Moonlight Graham played in 1905. It is a living part of history, like calico dresses, stone crockery, and threshing crews eating at outdoor tables. It continually reminds us of what it once was, like an Indian-head penny in a handful of new coins.

—W. P. KINSELLA
NOVELIST

The day Custer lost at the Little Bighorn, the Chicago White Sox beat the Cincinnati Red Legs, 3–2. Both teams wore knickers. And they're still wearin' them today.

—CHARLES O. FINLEY
EXECUTIVE, KANSAS CITY, OAKLAND, 1961–1980

The baseball mania has run its course. It has no future as a professional endeavor.

—*CINCINNATI GAZETTE*, 1870

[Night baseball]'s just a fad.
It'll never last after the novelty wears off.

—**ED BARROW**
MANAGER, 1903–1904, 1918–1920;
WON ONE PENNANT, ONE WORLD
SERIES; EXECUTIVE, 1917–1945;
HALL OF FAME

On turf the ball comes to me and says, "Catch me." On grass it says, "Look out, sucker."

—GREG PRYOR

INFIELDER, TEN SEASONS, 1976–1986

If a horse can't eat it, I don't want to play on it.

—DICK ALLEN
OUTFIELDER, 1963–1977

I don't know. I never
smoked artificial turf.

—DOUG RADER
**1967–1977; MANAGER, SEVEN
SEASONS, 1960s–1990s; COACH**
UPON BEING ASKED ABOUT THE
DIFFERENCE BETWEEN GRASS
AND ARTIFICIAL TURF. (BUT SEE
PAGE IX. ALSO ATTRIBUTED TO
TUG McGRAW.)

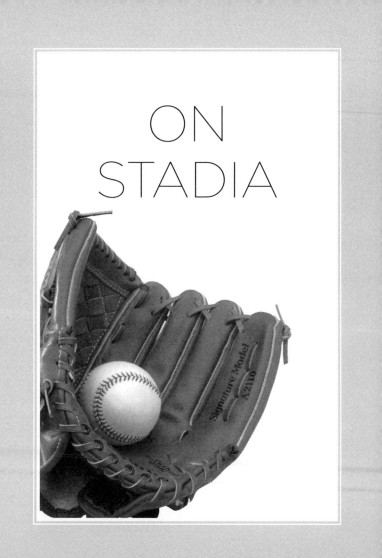

ON
STADIA

The view from Coogan's [the Polo Grounds] was gorgeous and beggared description. It was one of those perfect October days which so seldom come when you want them, and the landscape was like a [J. M. W.] Turner picture. The broad bosom of the Harlem River palpitated in the Autumn glow, the hazy blue of the Bronx draped the towering palaces along the heights overlooking the silver stream, the city to the south stretched away into limitless azure . . .

—W. J. LAMPTON
**SPORTSWRITER, *NEW YORK TIMES*,
OCT. 9, 1908**

At Fenway Park in 1912 the wall known today as the Green Monster had not yet been erected. Instead, there was a much lower wall carrying billboard ads for products such as Bull Durham tobacco. But the striking feature of this left-field region was an embankment which rose up in front of the wall, perhaps eight feet high, starting its rise about twenty-five feet from the fence. So the left fielder going back for a ball over his head had to run up this embankment while keeping his eye on the ball. . . . Duffy Lewis ordinarily played this hazardous terrain so well that the embankment became known as Duffy's Cliff.

—FRED LIEB
SPORTSWRITER

The damn thing [the left field wall at Fenway] is so close I scrape my knuckles on it every time I throw a sidearm curve.

—BOB FELLER

PITCHER, 17 SEASONS, 1936–1956; 266 LIFETIME WINS; HALL OF FAME

When I think of a stadium, it's like a temple. It's religious. Sometimes I'd go into Dodger Stadium just to be alone. The game might start at eight and I'd get there at one and sit in the stands and look at the field. It was that beautiful. No one would be there—only the birds chirping. And I'd see the sky and the grass. What a feeling!

—JIM LEFEBVRE
CATCHER, 1965–1972;
MANAGER, 1989–1993

Ebbets Field meant so much to me, even after I had left it to go to Yankee Stadium, that I never went back to look at the place after it became a ghost park. I have never gone back because I can still see Ebbets Field. As far as I am concerned, it is still standing.

—RED BARBER
SPORTSCASTER, AUTHOR

Even though many of its seats were unoccupied daily, Sportsman's Park was a marvel, both for the Cardinals and their fans. Cramped, warm, slightly homespun and lovably familiar, it reeked with memories and boundless nostalgia. Seats were hard, comforts uncommon, and parking was perpetually minute. Yet few were the seats which offered a poor view of the playing field; even the least expensive tickets made for intimate sport.

—CURT SMITH
SPORTSWRITER, BASEBALL
BIOGRAPHER

[Baker Bowl] was an atrocity, so far as baseball was concerned. It was built on one square city block and it was not a big block either. And the grandstands took up some space. The right field fence was 60 feet high while the playing surface was below the level of Lehigh Avenue which ran past it. The playing surface, I mean was 20 to 30 feet below street level, so the top of the fence was only about 30 feet above the street. They had a big sign on it which read "The Phillies Use Lifebuoy Soap."

—ANDY HIGH
INFIELDER, 1922–1934; COACH

I stand at the plate in Philadelphia [Veteran's Stadium] and I don't honestly know whether I'm in Pittsburgh, Cincinnati, St. Louis, or Philly. They all look alike.

—RICHIE HEBNER
INFIELDER, 1968–1985

The beautiful ivy vines on the [Wrigley Field] outfield wall provide plays such as Cub leftfielder Andy Pafko losing Tiger Roy Cullenbine's hit in the 1945 World Series and Roberto Clemente attempting to uncork one of his great throws to the plate with an empty white Coca-Cola cup.

—PHILIP J. LOWRY
BASEBALL HISTORIAN

ON
PROBLEMS

From its earliest days, baseball has indulged gamblers, fixers, drunkards, brawlers, disreputable moguls, bad actors, felons, homicidal maniacs, crooked umpires, vindictive owners, pyromaniacal fans, and at least one ax murderer.

—STEPHEN S. HALL
SCIENCE AND TRAVEL WRITER

The beanball is one of the meanest things on earth, and no decent fellow would use it. The beanball pitcher is a potential murderer. If I were a batter and thought that the pitcher really tried to bean me, I'd be inclined to wait for him outside the park with a baseball bat.

—WALTER JOHNSON
PITCHER, 1907–1927; 416 LIFETIME VICTORIES; MANAGER, 1929–1935; HALL OF FAME

It used to be "part of the game" to call all Jewish players Moe. It used to be part of the game to have no black players. It used to be part of the game for players to wear no protective headgear or catcher's gear. Baseball discarded these idiocies, but not the beanball.

—JIM KAPLAN

SPORTSWRITER, AUTHOR

I had the reputation of being the kind of pitcher who'd knock you down if you got a hit off me, but I wouldn't always do it on the first pitch. Maybe I'd throw you a knuckleball instead. Then a curveball. Then a nice change of pace. You'd start to think, Good, he forgot about that hit, and right then—whap—down you'd go. [Laughs delightedly.]

—LEON DAY
STAR PITCHER OF NEGRO LEAGUES;
HALL OF FAME

[Eddie Collins] seemed to have no sympathy for any of [the Black Sox], not even Jackson who was practically an illiterate, or young Buck Weaver who had been caught up in the polluted swirl of bad company, nor did he have any patience with the explanation that a penurious owner had shabbily under-paid hired hands.

"They were old enough to know the difference between right and wrong," he would say with cold level finality.

—JOE WILLIAMS
COLUMNIST, 1910s–1950s

It was like hearing that my church had sold out.

—BABE RUTH
PITCHER, OUTFIELDER, 1914–1935;
HIT 60 HOME RUNS IN 1927; 714
HOME RUNS LIFETIME; LIFETIME
.342 HITTER; COACH, 1938;
HALL OF FAME,
ON THE BLACK SOX SCANDAL

The extent of the involvement [of major league players in drugs] became pathetically clear when Montreal outfielder Tim Raines, the National League's leading base stealer, admitted that he often dove headfirst into second base during a steal so as to protect the gram bottle of cocaine he kept in his back pocket.

—STEPHEN S. HALL
SCIENCE AND TRAVEL WRITER

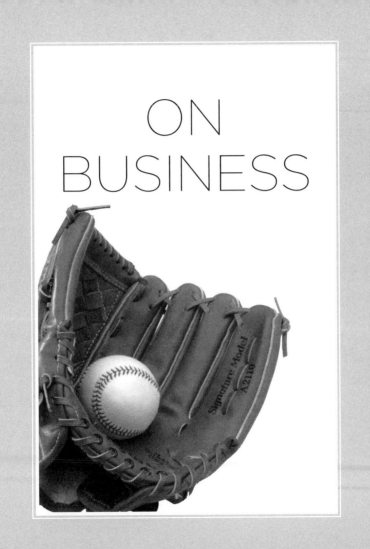

Indeed, at the 1869 Association convention Henry Chadwick admitted that baseball was a business, and teams on western barnstorming tours were regularly capitalizing on home-town boosterism and East-West rivalry (even as they spread interest in the game as well).

—JACK SELZER
UNIVERSITY PROFESSOR, AUTHOR

A common theme in baseball discussions from the late 1920s on was that ballplayers had started acting like bland businessmen—that they just didn't have the competitive spirit of the old-timers.

—CHARLES C. ALEXANDER
BASEBALL HISTORIAN,
BIOGRAPHER

If you're silly enough to give a back-up catcher seven hundred thousand dollars for two or three years, that's your problem.

—EDDIE MATHEWS

INFIELDER, 1952–1968; 512 LIFETIME HOME RUNS; MANAGER 1972–1974; HALL OF FAME

I've found out that in baseball they don't care a darn thing about you. Once you've stopped producing, you're gone. I went through this with the Cardinals. "You go along with us," they told me. "You'll always be with us, and we'll take care of you." The next year I was sold.

—JOHNNY MIZE
**INFIELDER, 15 SEASONS, 1936–1953;
HALL OF FAME**

There was a great deal of talk about the pension plan. I was with the Indians, and my teammate Bob Feller helped initiate the fight for the pension plan. (He's why it would later be operated out of Cleveland.) He was never given credit for what he did, but he was about the only big league ballplayer who stuck his neck out. Johnny Murphy did a good job, too. The pension plan would go into effect on April 1, but we put up the money in 1946. With one or two exceptions, every player and coach put up $300 apiece, and that was a lot of money for us just making $2,500 a year.

—GENE WOODLING
OUTFIELDER, 17 SEASONS,
1943–1962; COACH

Who determines this idea that athletes are overpaid? How much is "overpaid," anyway? If Elizabeth Taylor gets a million dollars for appearing in a picture, it adds to her attraction. Why isn't this true with ballplayers?

—TIM McCARVER
CATCHER, 1959–1980;
SPORTSCASTER; SPORTSWRITER

Ninety percent of
[my salary] I spent
on booze and women—
and the other ten
percent I wasted.

—TUG McGRAW

PITCHER, 1965–1984

ON
OWNERS

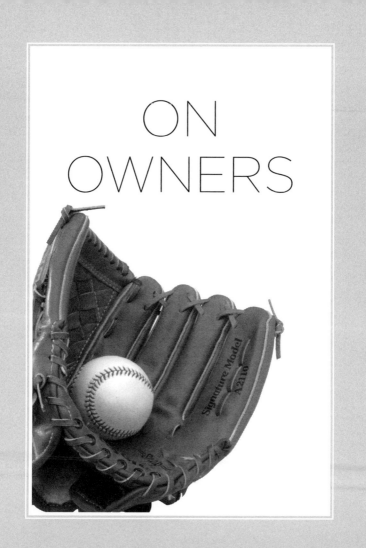

The greatest evil with which the business has of recent years to contend is the unscrupulous methods of some of its "managers." Knowing no such thing as professional honor, these men are ever ready to benefit themselves, regardless of the cost to an associate club. The reserve rule itself is a usurpation of the players' rights, but it is, perhaps, made necessary by the peculiar nature of the base-ball business, and the player is indirectly compensated by the improved standing of the game.

—JOHN MONTGOMERY WARD
PITCHER, INFIELDER, OUTFIELDER, 1878–1894; MANAGER. SEVEN SEASONS, 1880–1894; OWNER. 1912; HALL OF FAME

The reserve clause exists for two reasons. One, to cut down on the money the ballplayers get, and two, to give a feeling of power to men who like to play God over other people's lives.

—CURT FLOOD
OUTFIELDER, 15 YEARS, 1956–1971

Baseball—like our movies, like our newspapers and magazines—has fallen into the hands of rich, vulgar people who neither love nor understand it.

—HAL CROWTHER
SPORTSWRITER, COLUMNIST

I found out a long time ago that there is no charity in baseball, and that every owner must make his own fight for existence.

—JACOB RUPPERT
OWNER, NEW YORK YANKEES.
1915–1938

Mr. Breadon, if you ever threw $2,000 out the window, your arm would still be holding onto it.

—JOE MEDWICK
**OUTFIELDER, 1932–1948; .333
LIFETIME BATTING AVERAGE;
HALL OF FAME,**
TO SAM BREADON AT
CONTRACT TIME

There was something about [Branch Rickey] of the travelling medicine-show man, something of W. C. Fields. But his ultimate alteration of the game, the destruction of baseball's color bar, was an act of national significance—an essential remedy that had awaited a man of subtlety and stubborn moral courage to bring it about.

—ROGER ANGELL
AUTHOR, EDITOR

I couldn't tell Rickey to get better players because he was too pompous to allow us to talk to him about such matters.

—RALPH KINER
OUTFIELDER, 1946–1955; 369 LIFETIME HOME RUNS; SPORTSCASTER; HALL OF FAME

George [Steinbrenner] can't see that. Like I said, when he signs someone for big money, all of a sudden they become his bosom buddies, but the players who have been around for a year or two, he just thinks, Goddamn, they should be happy he's building the club, adding players to make the Yankees win again, that he's doing this for me, for Willie [Randolph], for whoever. But it isn't that way. No one wants to feel that he's being underpaid, I don't give a damn who you are, whether you're a truck driver, a secretary, or the president of General Motors.

—SPARKY LYLE
PITCHER, 1967–1982; 238 SAVES

It's a baseball fan's birthright to maintain a lifelong ambivalence toward the Yankees, respecting their great players while condemning an ownership that pays cash for its Ruths and Jacksons, brazenly buys players for every stretch, and regularly cashiers lovable old managers like Stengel and Lemon.

—THOMAS BOSWELL
SPORTSWRITER

[Marge] Schott and Steinbrenner are so disgusting the other owners had to pretend to punish them to keep the press and politicians at bay. They get the headlines. But don't overlook lower-profile swine like Jerry Reinsdorf of the Chicago White Sox, who methodically harassed and humiliated Carlton Fisk, the last of the old-time work-ethic ballplayers, and dumped him without apology at mid-season after 25 years in the game.

—HAL CROWTHER

SPORTSWRITER, COLUMNIST

In 1981, when George Steinbrenner was berating his Yankees after a loss in the playoffs against Milwaukee, one voice broke the silence with a brief rebuttal. "Go screw yourself, George." Catcher Rick Cerone, naturally.

—THOMAS BOSWELL
SPORTSWRITER

I've worked for Charlie [Finley]
and I've worked for George
Steinbrenner and I've survived
to tell about it. Not many others
can make that statement.

—EDDIE LOPAT
PITCHER, 1944–1955; MANAGER,
1963–1964

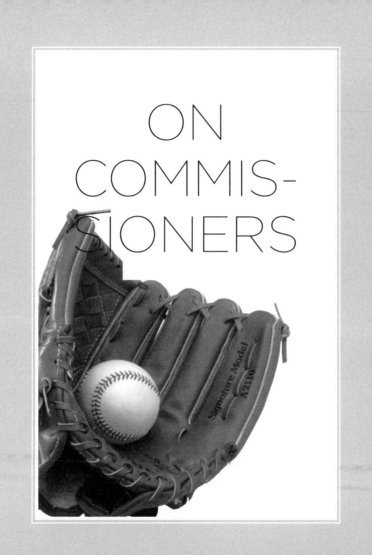

ON
COMMIS-
SIONERS

I think [Kenesaw Mountain Landis] was totally honest, but he was vain, egotistical, dominating, and a show-off. He swore like a trooper, chewed tobacco, and was fond of bourbon whiskey.

—FRED LIEB

SPORTSWRITER

If a black boy can make it on
Okinawa and Guadalcanal,
hell, he can make it in baseball.

—A. B. (HAPPY) CHANDLER
COMMISSIONER OF BASEBALL,
1945–1951; U. S. SENATOR

Owners have a duty to take into consideration that they own a part of America's national pastime in trust. This trust sometimes requires putting self-interest second.

—FAY VINCENT

COMMISSIONER OF BASEBALL,

1989–1992

ON
WIVES

Women are never no help around the ball club. Wives don't do no good.

—ROGERS HORNSBY
INFIELDER, 1915–1937; .358 LIFETIME
BATTING AVERAGE; MANAGER,
14 SEASONS, 1925–1937, 1952–1953;
HALL OF FAME

As a rule I do not approve a wife's accompanying her husband on the road trips. She seems to distract his attention.

—JOHN McGRAW

INFIELDER. 1891-1906; .344 LIFETIME BATTING AVERAGE; MANAGER. 33 YEARS, 1899-1932; WON TEN PENNANTS. THREE WORLD SERIES; HALL OF FAME

You can't even make love
to your husband when you
want to. You have to wait
for an off day.

—CYNDY (FORMERLY
MRS. STEVE) GARVEY

I don't know anything about baseball. That was Dizzy's business. But I do know how the money is to be got and what to do with it. When one member of the firm is lacking in practical sense it's a good thing the other member has it, and that's where I come in.

—PATRICIA DEAN
WIFE OF DIZZY DEAN

Mrs. [Laraine] Durocher was listening to my broadcast of a Brooklyn game. She got the word about Leo's new job with the Giants. Without hesitation she snapped off the radio with the remark, "What am I listening to this for?"

—RED BARBER

SPORTSCASTER, AUTHOR

That old Dodger club was very close. Most of us had been together for a number of years, and when we'd gather in the clubhouse that first day of spring training, it was like when you were a kid going back to school in the fall with all your school friends. We could hardly wait.

Our wives once in a while got a little jealous because we spent so much time together. Lots of times after a road game, ten or fifteen of us would go out and spend the evenings together.

—DUKE SNIDER
OUTFIELDER, 1947–1967; 407
LIFETIME HOME RUNS; COACH,
1974–1975; HALL OF FAME

When I first got to know Satchel Paige, he had a wife whose nickname was Toad. She was a barmaid at the Grand Hotel in Chicago, and when we played the Chicago American Giants, we would go there after the game. We'd say, "Hey, Toad! Where's Satchel?" "You asking me where Satchel is?" she'd say. "I should be asking you. I haven't seen him in weeks. If you see him, tell him to give me a call."

—MONTE IRVIN
STAR IN NEGRO LEAGUES;
INFIELDER, OUTFIELDER, 1949–1956;
HALL OF FAME

A ballplayer gets so used to everybody treating him well and looking after him that he begins to expect that at home. I was just telling Bernie today that he can't expect the same treatment at home that he gets out here at the ballpark.

—WALESKA (MRS. BERNIE) WILLIAMS

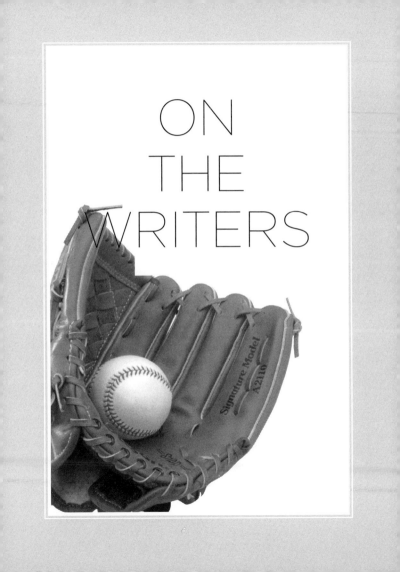

ON
THE
WRITERS

You could always tell a player's worth by the space given to his obit in the *Sporting News*, and Taylor [Spink] gave me the big ones. I covered the passing of the real greats, Nap Lajoie, Hans Wagner, Bobby Wallace, Walter Johnson, Paul Waner, Grover Cleveland Alexander, Mickey Cochrane, and dozens of others. I wrote so many of these "last rites" that Bob Broeg, the gifted baseball writer and sports editor of the *St. Louis Post-Dispatch*, dubbed me the "baseball undertaker."

—FRED LIEB
SPORTSWRITER

When I entered the game we received only a few lines as news. These few lines expanded into columns and pages; in ratio the crowds in our ball parks grew and grew and grew. News, like advertising, is a powerful momentum behind any enterprise.

The professional sporting world was created and is being kept alive by the services extended by the press.

—CONNIE MACK
CATCHER, 1886–1896; MANAGER, 53 SEASONS, 1894–1950; WON EIGHT PENNANTS, FIVE WORLD SERIES; HALL OF FAME

One of the most famous paragraphs in baseball literature was the one the late John Lardner wrote: "Floyd Caves Herman never tripled into a triple play, but he once doubled into a double play, which is the next best thing."

—JIM MURRAY

BASEBALL COLUMNIST, EDITOR

The Colts were beaten and rained upon, in that order, at Mooers Field yesterday.

—SHELLEY ROLFE

SPORTSWRITER, COLUMNIST

(MY ALL-TIME FAVORITE LEAD SENTENCE ABOUT A BASEBALL GAME, WRITTEN ABOUT THE RICHMOND COLTS OF THE OLD PIEDMONT LEAGUE, IN THE RICHMOND, VA., *TIMES-DISPATCH*, C. 1948)

I'm always amazed at the amount of hostility among the male writers that is directed at the players. Obviously, not all the writers are failed athletes, but there are far too many of them.

—STEPHANIE SALTER
SPORTSWRITER

Writers don't fire managers. Losses fire managers. Writers, even the self-absorbed ones who think of themselves as poets, baseball gurus, or press box Woodwards and Bernsteins, don't make a team lose. They might make teams miserable or uptight, but they ultimately don't make teams lose.

—PETER PASCARELLI
SPORTSWRITER, BASEBALL HISTORIAN

You tell [Charles] Dryden [of the *New York American*] that he is standing on the brink of an abscess and if he ain't careful, I'll push him in.

—ANDREW FREEDMAN
OWNER, NEW YORK GIANTS,
1895–1902; TAMMANY POLITICO

Ballplayers shouldn't gripe about reporters. A ballplayer should stay on a reporter's good side. Say nice things. Admire his clothes. Compliment him on his t-shirt.

—ANDY VAN SLYKE
OUTFIELDER, 1983–1995

It was just before Opening Day and an earnest New York baseball writer asked, "Leo, do you intend to get your team off to a fast start this year?" Durocher looked at him contemptuously and rasped, "No, you stupid son of a bitch, I'm gonna lose the first ten games."

—ROBERT W. CREAMER

SPORTSWRITER, BIOGRAPHER, EDITOR

After [Don Larsen's perfect game in the 1956 World Series], manager Casey Stengel was asked the dumbest question in the history of journalism: Was that the best game he had ever seen Larsen pitch? Stengel said: "So far."

—GEORGE F. WILL
COLUMNIST

I can still hear Pete Rose, on the top of the dugout screaming, "Fuck you, Shakespeare."

—JIM BOUTON
PITCHER, 1962–1970, 1978; AUTHOR,
AFTER PUBLICATION OF HIS BOOK
BALL FOUR

Jimmy [Cannon]'s spoken lines were as swift and pointed as the ones he wrote. At a World Series he was scolding about Baltimore fans—he was capable of throwing a hate on a whole city— and a press box companion demurred: "Oh, Jimmy, people are alike every- where." "Like Francis of Assisi and Adolf Eichmann?" he shot back.

—RED SMITH
COLUMNIST

The most stupid ball player knows more, really, about the game than any baseball writer I ever knew.

—JOHN KIERAN
COLUMNIST, ESSAYIST;
OUTFIELDER, 1946–1955; 369
LIFETIME HOME RUNS;
SPORTSCASTER; HALL OF FAME

Now, a World Series is a big thrill for a young baseball writer and for a baseball fan of any age, but for dotards like me it is just a golden opportunity to sit around and discuss the game as it was before Mr. Volstead substituted the lively ball for Schlitz in brown bottles.

—RING LARDNER
SPORTSWRITER, AUTHOR,
HUMORIST

From my experience as a ghostwriter,
I know that eventually the writer must
fly solo. Assuming that the Babe tired,
as most athletes do, it is necessary for
the ghost to go the distance.

—JEROME HOLTZMAN
SPORTSWRITER, EDITOR,
ON FORD FRICK'S ROLE IN *BABE
RUTH'S OWN BOOK OF BASEBALL*

Joe, thanks for not trading me.

—JIM BUNNING
PITCHER, 1955–1971; 224 LIFETIME WINS; HALL OF FAME, TO JOE FALLS AFTER THE DETROIT COLUMNIST WROTE ABOUT VARIOUS TRADES THAT THE TIGERS SHOULD MAKE

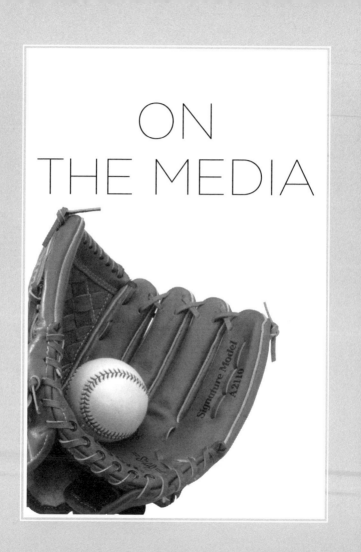

ON
THE MEDIA

Joe Garagiola on NBC television is today the fountain of all wisdom and knowledge. Woe to the player who makes a "head" mistake. Joe at length explains how the play should have been made, and how much the oversight cost the erring player's team. The "dumb" play is meat and potatoes for Garagiola, and what he doesn't criticize, his partner Tony Kubek does.

—RED BARBER
SPORTSCASTER, AUTHOR

You know what some of these advertising guys are trying to do? They're trying to get Diz to speak English.

—PATRICIA DEAN
WIFE OF DIZZY DEAN

"There's a word for what television's turned this game into."

"What's the word?"

"Beans," he said. "Nothing but beans and hot air."

—WILLIAM LEAST HEAT MOON
AUTHOR

Would you say, Harvey, that this is the best game you ever pitched?

—PITTSBURGH RADIO ANNOUNCER,
AFTER HARVEY HADDIX PITCHED
A PERFECT GAME FOR 12 INNINGS,
ONLY TO LOSE BY 1–0 IN THE 13TH

When I said I was going to quit, Lylah [Barber], a very wise woman, said, "You don't have to quit tonight. You can do that tomorrow. . . . Let's have a martini."

—RED BARBER

SPORTSCASTER, AUTHOR, AFTER LEARNING FROM BRANCH RICKEY THAT HE INTENDED TO BRING A BLACK PLAYER INTO MAJOR LEAGUE BASEBALL

The rain is coming down hard now. Although I guess the real story would be if the rain was going up.

—TOMMY HUTTON
INFIELDER, 12 SEASONS,
1966–1979; SPORTSCASTER.
ANNOUNCING A YANKEE GAME

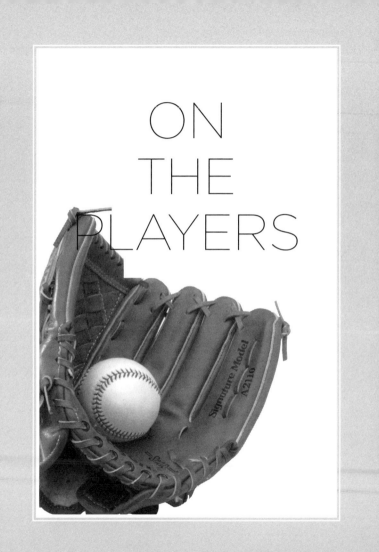

ON
THE
PLAYERS

Photos of Aaron hitting homers baffled coaches. As the ball left his bat, his back foot was completely off the ground, all his weight was far forward, and—horror of horrors—his right hand flew off the bat an instant after contact, creating the illusion that he was swinging at the ball one-handed, almost throwing the bat at the ball.

—THOMAS BOSWELL
SPORTSWRITER

The pitcher only had a ball, I had a bat.

—HENRY AARON
OUTFIELDER, 1954–1976;
LIFETIME 755 HOME RUNS, 2,297
RBI; HALL OF FAME

What's the use of doin'
in three pitches what
you can do in one?

—GROVER CLEVELAND ALEXANDER
**PITCHER, 1911–1930; WON 373
GAMES; HALL OF FAME**

Mays, Mantle, and Maris . . . but I saw Dick Allen. He was the best, just unbelievable.

—GOOSE GOSSAGE
PITCHER, 1972–1994; 310 SAVES

He was a low-key manager that let his team play; he didn't act like he was the only one who could win or lose a game, like Billy Martin did.

—QV LOWE
SCOUT, COACH

I saw right away that he was one of the nicest people in the game. And I could see that he could play.

—HANK SAUER
OUTFIELDER, 15 YEARS, 1941-1959;
COACH

I'll say this, going from first to home, Jesse [Owens] wouldn't have beaten Cool Papa [Bell]. Cool Papa was the fastest man I've ever seen. He was faster than Maury Wills and Lou Brock and Mickey Mantle when Mickey had good legs. He was faster than Bo Jackson and Kenny Lofton.

—BUCK O'NEIL
STAR PLAYER, MANAGER IN NEGRO
LEAGUES; COACH; SCOUT

He came to the fore when the much smaller hinged catching mitt first became popular, and his shortstop-quick hands and his smoothness and balance and mobility behind the plate instantly caused all the catchers in the land to imitate his one-handed style, but none of them, then or now, could touch him.

—ROGER ANGELL
AUTHOR, EDITOR

Soon after I got traded to Baltimore, I came up to play in New York. Yogi [Berra] was the catcher, Eddie Rommel was the umpire, and I was the batter. I was trying to concentrate when I hear, "Hey, Gene, did you know Carmen's pregnant?" Rommel busted up. Yogi was serious, not trying to distract me. That was Yogi.

—GENE WOODLING
OUTFIELDER, 17 SEASONS,
1943–1962; COACH

"Bill [Dickey] is learning me all his experiences."

—YOGI BERRA
CATCHER, 1946–1965; 358 HOME
RUNS; MANAGER, 1964, 1972–1975,
1984–1985; COACH; HALL OF FAME

I ain't bragging about myself or anything like that, but I got to admit I'm the only real ballplayer Connie [Mack]'s got. I and the Liberty Bell are the only attractions left in Philadelphia.

—PING BODIE
OUTFIELDER, NINE SEASONS, 1911–1921

And, best of all, George Brett batting, a
brilliant repeated exhibit of precision and
style and success.

—ROGER ANGELL
AUTHOR, EDITOR

There was a limit to how much I could fit in. I was a good cook, but I wasn't going to discuss fine cuisine with another player. I wasn't going to ask any of the players to go with me to see Vladimir Horowitz in concert. I wasn't going to ask Bill Henry to come over and listen to Mahler. I never met anybody in baseball who liked classical music to the extent that I did. If they saw the ecstasy on my face they would have wondered what was wrong with me.

—JIM BROSNAN
PITCHER, NINE SEASONS, 1954–1963;
AUTHOR; SPORTSCASTER

Mordecai, Mordecai, Mordecai Brown!

How come you goin' aroun' and aroun'?

"I heard the Yellow Pages talking:

'Let your fingers do the walking.'"

—WILLIAM HARMON
POET, CRITIC

I'd like to have a buck for every time I was called a "crazy left-hander" by somebody. How many times have you ever heard somebody called a "crazy right-hander"? That's discrimination. You ever see a left-handed water fountain? There you are.

—TOMMY BYRNE
PITCHER, 13 YEARS, 1943–1957

He'll have a three-ball, two-strike count on him and foul off six consecutive pitches. Then he'll finally let one go. Well, if he swung at six and didn't swing at that one, it's got to be ball four. The great hitters get treated that way because they've proven they know the strike zone. If Ted Williams didn't swing at a pitch, it was a ball, wherever it was.

—RON LUCIANO
UMPIRE, 1968–1980; AUTHOR

Sometimes I hit him like I used to hit [Sandy] Koufax, and that's like drinking coffee with a fork.

—WILLIE STARGELL
OUTFIELDER. INFIELDER. 1962–1982;
475 HOME RUNS; COACH;
HALL OF FAME

After a game lost this season Chance yelled at his men, "You're a fine lot of curs, you are." Not exactly the kind of talk boys expect from their fathers. Rumor has it that "curs" was not the word used, but it will do under the circumstances.

—*NEW YORK EVENING MAIL*,
JULY 24, 1908

But the greatest ball player I've ever seen in my life was Oscar Charleston. I'd rate Oscar Charleston over Joe DiMaggio, over Willie Mays.

—TED PAGE
OUTFIELD STAR OF NEGRO
LEAGUES

If only I could calcimine him.

—JOHN McGRAW
INFIELDER, 1891–1906; .344
LIFETIME BATTING AVERAGE;
MANAGER, 33 YEARS, 1899–1932;
WON TEN PENNANTS, THREE
WORLD SERIES; HALL OF FAME

Sometimes he forgets that he's a human being. I have to remind him that even a pitching machine throws a bad one every once in a while.

—BILL FISCHER
PITCHER, 1956–1964; COACH

He looked like he was falling apart when he ran. Looked like he was coming apart when he threw. His stance at the plate was ridiculous. When he swung he'd lunge and hit bad balls. There was no way he could hit the ball like that. But no one told Roberto that.

—ROBIN ROBERTS
PITCHER, 1948–1966; WON 245
GAMES; HALL OF FAME

Thank goodness Al they ain't no Cobbs in this league and a man ain't scared of haveing his uniform stole off his back.

—RING LARDNER
SPORTSWRITER, AUTHOR, HUMORIST

The greatest ballplayer I ever saw?
Well, I'll have to say Ty Cobb. He could
do more with a bat than any player of
my time and I don't suppose there ever
was a base runner like him. They tell
you he wasn't much of a fielder, but he
was good enough. I know he took a lot
of base hits from me out there.

—BABE RUTH
PITCHER, OUTFIELDER, 1914–1935;
HIT 60 HOME RUNS IN 1927;
714 HOME RUNS LIFETIME;
LIFETIME .342 HITTER; COACH, 1938;
HALL OF FAME

His foremost rival, Babe Ruth, had died in 1948 and an estimated quarter of a million people filed by his coffin at Yankee Stadium. The beloved Babe packed St. Patrick's Cathedral and every major-league club was represented at the two-day services. Ty Cobb drew just three men from big-league ball to his funeral. They were Mickey Cochrane, old-time catcher Ray Schalk, and Nap Rucker from his minor-league days.

—AL STUMP
SPORTSWRITER, BIOGRAPHER

I don't think the fires ever went out in him, not till the day he died.

—OSSIE BLUEGE
INFIELDER, 1922–1939; MANAGER, 1943–1947; COACH

Players he had competed with and against did not visit him at Atherton in any number. Fred Haney, who had played with the Tigers, told of leaving a Detroit game with Cobb one evening in the mid-1940s and encountering players waiting for taxis. The boys were play-wrestling and laughing. "I wish I could have done that," said Cobb wistfully. "Had some pals on the team and kept them. But I didn't."

—AL STUMP

SPORTSWRITER, BIOGRAPHER

I went up and singled to left, driving in the winning run. Cy [Perkins] took off his catching equipment just as the man crossed the plate, the boys on the bench told me much later, and said, "There goes Perkins' job on that base hit." I caught 135 that season.

—MICKEY COCHRANE
CATCHER, 1925–1937;
.320 LIFETIME BATTING AVERAGE;
MANAGER, 1934–1938; WON TWO
PENNANTS, ONE WORLD SERIES;
HALL OF FAME

[Ray Schalk said that] after Eddie Collins came to the White Sox in 1915, he became a better catcher. "Collins always caught the signal for a steal and gave me the sign. All I had to do was throw the ball to second base."

—JAMES T. FARRELL
NOVELIST

Sitting on the bench, Bobby Cox looks so aggravated on almost every play in a big game that you can't help but worry about his health. We once cut back from an antacid commercial to show the Braves' manager grimacing, and my quip was too easy: "The Battle of Mylanta."

—TIM McCARVER
CATCHER, 1959–1980;
SPORTSCASTER; SPORTSWRITER

I made an appearance on the "Good Morning, America" show. [The announcer] said, "You know Whitey Ford had a good curve ball."

I told him, "I know Whitey Ford had one of the best curve balls. But I had one of the best bats."

—RAY DANDRIDGE
STAR INFIELDER, NEGRO LEAGUES,
1933–1948; HALL OF FAME

The Good Lord was good to me. He gave me a good body, a strong right arm and a weak mind.

—DIZZY DEAN

**PITCHER, 1930–1938;
SPORTSCASTER; HALL OF FAME**

By Judas Priest! By Judas Priest!
If there were more like him in
baseball, just one, as God is my
witness, I'd get out of the game.

—BRANCH RICKEY
CATCHER, 1905-1907, 1914;
MANAGER, TEN SEASONS, 1913-1925;
EXECUTIVE, 1910s-1950s;
PIONEERED IN FARM SYSTEM;
ENDED RACIAL SEGREGATION
IN PROFESSIONAL BASEBALL;
HALL OF FAME

X-RAYS OF DEAN'S HEAD SHOW NOTHING

—HEADLINE IN DETROIT NEWSPAPER
AFTER DIZZY DEAN WAS HIT BY
THROWN BASEBALL IN 1934
WORLD SERIES

DeHigo was the greatest all-round player I know. I say he was the best ball player of all time, black or white. He could do it all.

—BUCK LEONARD

STAR INFIELDER IN NEGRO LEAGUES, 1933–1950; HALL OF FAME

He was a great fellow to work with. He was real patient with a young pitcher, he'd always encourage you, and he seemed to know what to call for.

—SPUD CHANDLER
PITCHER, 1937–1947

They [Joe DiMaggio and Marilyn Monroe] had been married in January of that year, 1954, despite disharmony in temperament and time: he was tired of publicity, she was thriving on it; he was intolerant of tardiness, she was always late. During their honeymoon in Tokyo, an American general had introduced himself and asked if, as a patriotic gesture, she would visit the troops in Korea. She looked at Joe. "It's your honeymoon," he said, shrugging, "go ahead if you want to."

She appeared on ten occasions before 100,000 servicemen, and when she returned she said, "It was so wonderful, Joe. You never heard such cheering."

"Yes I have," he said.

—GAY TALESE
AUTHOR

He was the greatest
living ballplayer I've
ever seen play.

—YOGI BERRA
CATCHER, 1946–1965; 358 HOME
RUNS; MANAGER, 1964, 1972–1975,
1984–1985; COACH; HALL OF FAME

We were in the Oriole pen and it was about the sixth inning of the game. Jim Nash was pitching a two-hit shutout against us, just breezing. It wasn't really a premeditated thing on my part but I called over to their pen to find out what players were in the doghouse, whose wives were expecting babies, just get caught up on all the local news. When their coach, a fellow named Bobby Hofman, picked up the phone, I don't know why but I hollered, "Get Krausse hot in a hurry!" and hung up the phone. All of a sudden two bodies came charging out of the bullpen and they proceeded to heat up. Nash is still cruising along on this two-hitter and he looks down there and wonders what the hell is going on. So I let them throw for a while and then called back and said, "That's enough, sit 'em down."

—MOE DRABOWSKY
PITCHER, 1956–1972

I knocked down a lot of people but I can honestly say I never hit anybody in the head.

—DON DRYSDALE
**209 LIFETIME WINS;
SPORTSCASTER; HALL OF FAME**

I have never questioned the
integrity of an umpire. Their
eyesight, yes.

—LEO DUROCHER

INFIELDER, 17 YEARS, 1925–1945;
MANAGER, 24 YEARS, 1939–1973;
WON THREE PENNANTS, ONE
WORLD SERIES; HALL OF FAME

Durocher tried to intimidate the other team with this kind of rough stuff, but I think it backfired on him more often than not. He was just stirring up a nest of hornets. When Durocher came to town I was so charged up before the game, man, I could go out there and climb six fences. And I wasn't the only one. Our whole team was up.

—STAN MUSIAL
OUTFIELDER, INFIELDER, 22 SEASONS, 1941–1963; .331 LIFETIME BATTING AVERAGE, 475 HOME RUNS; HALL OF FAME

It's also true that Dressen talks too much, mostly in sentences beginning with "I," "I'm," or "I'll." (It should be remembered that he spent some of his formative days in the Three-I League.)

—JOHN LARDNER
SPORTSWRITER, COLUMNIST

The Cardinals and the Indians had an exhibition game in Cleveland. Feller was warming up and couldn't find home-plate. He was throwing the ball all over the place. Frankie Frisch, the St. Louis manager and second baseman, was a close observer of these proceedings. All of a sudden he turns to one of the utility infielders and says, "I don't feel so good today; you're playing second."

—TONY PIET
INFIELDER, 1931–1938

Fidrych's mother's parting words to him when he signed a pro contract were "You make sure you come home the same nut you've always been."

—THOMAS BOSWELL
SPORTSWRITER

That was one thing you could count on with Whitey—he'd never make the same mistake twice. For a young fellow he was fantastic.

—ED LOPAT
PITCHER, 1944–1955; MANAGER, 1963–1964

Oh no, he hasn't got a thing. I just thought he was shooting at me with a rifle when I was up there.

—PERCY WERDEN

LONGTIME PLAYER IN NEGRO LEAGUES

He had great powerful arms, and he used to wear his sleeves cut off way up, and when he dug in and raised that bat, those muscles would bulge and ripple.

—TED LYONS
PITCHER. 21 SEASONS, 1923-1946;
260 LIFETIME WINS; HALL OF FAME

When they start speaking of second base-ing in particular, and bragging of the way second base is played in their time—Tell them About Frisch.

Tell 'em most especially about the way Frisch played second base, some of center field and a slice of right field, too . . .

—DAMON RUNYON
AUTHOR, HUMORIST

I have a wonderful wife. I have a wonderful father and mother, and wonderful friends and teammates. I have been privileged to play many years with the famous Yankees, the greatest team of all times. All in all, I can say on this day that I consider myself the luckiest man on the face of the earth.

—LOU GEHRIG
INFIELDER, 1923–1939; 493 HOME RUNS, 1,990 RBI; PLAYED IN 2,130 CONSECUTIVE GAMES; HALL OF FAME, ON LOU GEHRIG DAY, JULY 4, 1939, YANKEE STADIUM, TWO YEARS BEFORE HIS DEATH AT AGE 38

Solly [Hemus] also didn't like Bob Gibson. I don't think it was a black and white thing. He complained, "Bob throws every pitch at the same speed." That's like saying an atomic bomb explodes at the same velocity every time, so you can't use it.

—TIM McCARVER
CATCHER, 1959–1980;
SPORTSCASTER; SPORTSWRITER

Who was the hardest hitter for me to pitch against? That's him: Josh Gibson. He could hit home runs around Babe Ruth's home runs. You look for his weakness, and while you're looking for it, he's liable to hit 45 home runs.

—SATCHEL PAIGE
PITCHING STAR AND BEST-KNOWN
PLAYER IN NEGRO LEAGUES;
ENTERED MAJOR LEAGUES AT
AGE 42; PITCHER, FIVE YEARS,
1948–1953; HALL OF FAME

You couldn't fool him—don't think you're gonna fool him. Josh will hit you with one hand as quick as he will with two. I've seen him reach out on a sharp-breaking curveball on the outside from a right-hand pitcher, almost fooled him—almost. The ball almost got by him, and he reached out with one hand and hit it over the right field fence. And he ran the bases hollering, "Ha, you like to fooled me that time, but don't try that no more."

—VERDELL MATHIS
LONGTIME PITCHING STAR IN
NEGRO LEAGUES

I wanted to win this game as badly as any in my life, but I felt I had to fight my emotions and keep my ego in check.

—TOM GLAVINE
PITCHER, 1987–,
ON LETTING MARK WOHLERS PITCH
THE NINTH INNING OF THE
DECIDING GAME OF THE 1995
WORLD SERIES FOR ATLANTA

I owe my baseball success to clean living and a fast outfield.

—LEFTY GOMEZ

PITCHER, 1930–1943; HALL OF FAME

Well, it was a great honor to win a batting title in those days. It wasn't an easy thing to do.

—GOOSE GOSLIN
OUTFIELDER, 1921–1938; .316
LIFETIME BATTING AVERAGE;
HALL OF FAME

I was much more disappointed when I failed to break Gehrig's runs-batted-in record in 1937 then I was when I didn't break Babe Ruth's home-run record in 1938. Runs batted in were my obsession, not home runs.

—HANK GREENBERG

INFIELDER, OUTFIELDER, 12 SEASONS, 1933–1947; 331 HOME RUNS, 1,276 RBI; HALL OF FAME

Here's this minor-league pitcher throwing nothing but fastballs and blowing them right past everybody. They knew what they were going to get, but it didn't make any difference. Somebody said, "Well, he'll never make it in the big league. All he can do is throw a fastball." And somebody else said, "Yeah, and all Galli-Curci can do is sing."

—**TED LYONS**
PITCHER, 21 SEASONS, 1923–1946;
260 LIFETIME WINS; HALL OF FAME

He's going to get his hits and you just
hope no one's on base. He has such a
short, compact swing and such a good
idea of the strike zone that you are not
going to fool him very often. Out of
650 at bats in a season you will fool
him maybe ten times.

—MIKE LAVALLIERE
CATCHER, 1984–1995

I am the captain of the outfield.

—RICKEY HENDERSON

OUTFIELDER. 1979– ; 1,297 STOLEN
BASES THROUGH 1998

"Did you ever pitch much to Rogers Hornsby, Red?" I asked [Red Faber].

"I struck him out. It was at an old-timers game at Comiskey Park."

"Yes," Ray Schalk remarked, "and Lefty Gomez on the bench said, 'After twenty-five years we learned how to pitch to him.'"

—JAMES T. FARRELL
NOVELIST

I hit .361, played second base, and managed the club on two western trips. What does a fellow have to do to stay in New York?

—ROGERS HORNSBY
INFIELDER, 1915–1937; .358 LIFETIME
BATTING AVERAGE; MANAGER,
14 SEASONS, 1925–1937, 1952–1953;
HALL OF FAME,
UPON BEING TRADED BY THE
GIANTS TO THE BOSTON BRAVES

Houk tried to look comfortable in his new role [as Yankees' general manager], but mostly he looked out of place, or as one player said, "like a whore in church."

—JIM BOUTON
PITCHER, 1962–1970, 1978: AUTHOR

Well, it would be kinda hard to answer that because Nolan Ryan won't be pitching against Ruth, Gehrig, Foxx, Simmons, and Cronin.

—CARL HUBBELL

PITCHER, 1928–1943; 253 WINS LIFETIME; HALL OF FAME, AT THE 1979 ALL-STAR GAME, UPON BEING ASKED WHETHER HE THOUGHT RYAN COULD EQUAL HIS FEAT OF STRIKING OUT IN ORDER THE FIVE LEADING HITTERS IN THE AMERICAN LEAGUE LINEUP OF 1934

I'll tell you something about Hubbell. When he was pitching, you hardly ever saw the opposing team sitting back in the dugout; they were all up on the top step, watching him operate. He was a marvel to watch, with that screwball, fastball, curve, screwball again, change of speed, control. He didn't really have overpowering stuff, but he was an absolute master of what he did have, and he got every last ounce out of his abilities.

—BILLY HERMAN
INFIELDER, 15 YEARS, 1931–1947;
MANAGER, 1947, 1964–1966; COACH;
HALL OF FAME

Jackson never seemed to know whether the pitcher was left-handed or right, or whether he hit a fastball, curve, a spitter, or any of the trick deliveries. All he'd say, if you asked him, was that the ball was over. 'Over' for Jackson meant anything he could reach.

—JACK GRANEY
INFIELDER, 1908–1922

For Shoeless Joe is gone, long gone,

A long yellow grass-blade between
his teeth

And the bleacher shadows behind him

—NELSON ALGREN
NOVELIST

Joe Jackson's not alive any more. He's served his sentence, and it's time for baseball to acknowledge his debt is paid; and the Hall of Fame Committee on Veterans to list him as a nominee.

—TED WILLIAMS
OUTFIELDER, 19 YEARS, 1939–1960;
.344 LIFETIME BATTING AVERAGE,
521 HOMERS; MANAGER, 1969–1972;
HIT .406 IN 1941; HALL OF FAME

I represent both the underdog and the overdog in our society.

—REGGIE JACKSON

OUTFIELDER, 1967–1987; 563 HOME RUNS; HALL OF FAME

Another time Reggie [Jackson] was giving Mickey Rivers the same jive. "My IQ is 160," he told Mickey. Mickey looked at Reggie and said, "Out of what, Buck, a thousand?"

—SPARKY LYLE
PITCHER, 1967–1982; 238 SAVES

All I ever wanted to be was a Yankee. When I was a kid I was always hoping there'd be a jersey left for me to wear with a single digit.

—DEREK JETER
INFIELDER, 1995–,
WHO WEARS NO. 2

[Randy Johnson] long had been the kind of natural wonder better suited to an Ansel Adams portrait than a baseball card.

—TOM VERDUCCI
SPORTSWRITER

Didn't even have a curve. Just that fast ball. That's all he pitched, just fast balls. He didn't need any curve.

—SAM CRAWFORD

OUTFIELDER, 1899–1917; 1,525 RBI;
HALL OF FAME

He had what I would describe as a slingshot delivery. It was a nice, easy movement, which didn't seem to be putting any strain at all on his arm. But he could propel that ball like a bullet.

—FRED LINDSTROM
INFIELDER, 1924-1936; .311 LIFETIME
BATTING AVERAGE; HALL OF FAME

It was then that the great Master of
the Universe took the star twirler
out of the box and sent him to the
clubhouse . . .

—THE REV. BILLY SUNDAY
~~OUTFIELDER, 1883–1890;~~
REVIVALIST,
FUNERAL SERMON FOR
ADDIE JOSS, TOLEDO, OHIO, 1911

I knew that [Art Houtteman] was stubborn enough to test his fastball against me although I was a good fastball hitter. So on the first pitch I guessed correctly that he'd challenge me with his best fastball down the middle. I jumped all over it and drilled it for a double off the wall. As I glided into second, Art looked at me and said, "You really can hit a fastball, Cap'n."

—GEORGE KELL
INFIELDER, 1943–1957;
SPORTSCASTER; HALL OF FAME

All at once Sandy got control. And I don't mean control in the sense of just throwing the ball over the plate. He could throw the fastball where he wanted to—to spots. When you have that kind of stuff and that kind of control, well, they just stopped hitting him. And it all happened in one year.

—WALTER ALSTON
PITCHER, 1936; MANAGER
1954–1976; FINISHED FIRST SEVEN
TIMES, WON FOUR WORLD SERIES;
HALL OF FAME

Trying to sneak a fastball past him was like trying to sneak a sunrise past a rooster.

—MONTE IRVIN
STAR IN NEGRO LEAGUES;
INFIELDER, OUTFIELDER, 1949-1956;
HALL OF FAME

SPARKY LYLE

I remember one day before a game, [Bill] Virdon called a team meeting to go over the hitters. We were playing Baltimore, and Fred Stanley had gotten a casket from a guy in the business, an economy one with white silk, silver sprayed. It was finished inside, and Fred was going to make a bar out of it for his van. When he got it, he brought it into the clubhouse and kept it there until he could ship it home. It was sitting on a hand truck in the middle of the room. Well, I had gotten a surgical mask from a friend of mine. It had a hood that fit over your head, and all you could see were your eyes. I got lampblack and put it around my eyes and got them real black. Before the meeting started, I laid down inside the casket and shut it. I was listening, and Bill was going over the Baltimore lineup, and all of a sudden I lifted the top of the casket and said, "How dooooooo yooooooo pitch to Brooks Ro—been—son?"

—SPARKY LYLE
PITCHER, 1967–1982; 238 SAVES

Connie entered professional baseball when it was a game for roughnecks. He saw it become respectable, he lived to be a symbol of its integrity, and he enjoyed every minute of it.

—RED SMITH
COLUMNIST

He doesn't seem dominating, then you look up on the scoreboard and you've got one hit and it's the eighth inning.

—JIM THOME
INFIELDER, 1991–

We sometimes seem to save our greatest devotion for those heroes who don't quite make it, or who lose gallantly, or who have flaws. Mantle more than fit the image.

—ROBERT W. CREAMER
SPORTSWRITER, BIOGRAPHER, EDITOR

That boy hits balls over buildings. He runs as fast as Ty Cobb.

—CASEY STENGEL
OUTFIELDER, 1912–1925; MANAGER,
1934–1943, 1949–1960, 1962–1965;
WON TEN PENNANTS, SEVEN
WORLD SERIES, FIVE IN A ROW;
COACH; HALL OF FAME

But the best pitcher I ever batted against was Juan Marichal, because he threw so many goddam different kinds of good pitches against you.

—PETE ROSE
INFIELDER, OUTFIELDER, 1963–1986;
SET LIFETIME RECORDS OF 3,562
MAJOR LEAGUE GAMES PLAYED,
14,053 TIMES AT BAT, 4,256 BASE
HITS; MANAGER, 1984–1986;
BANNED FROM BASEBALL IN
1989 FOR GAMBLING

Sooner or later he'd get around to the game he liked best to recall. It was against the Pirates, always a soft touch for him. "Just get me one run," he told his teammates. "That's all I need to beat these guys."

It was tied until the 21st when Larry Doyle hit an inside-the-park homer. "Next time you say you need only one run to win," laughed Larry, "be specific. Name the inning."

—JOE WILLIAMS
COLUMNIST, 1910s–1950s

Martin was "tendency-prone," but he had so many tendencies it was hard to predict what he would do next.

—GEORGE F. WILL
COLUMNIST

We were put out of hotels in other cities, too. The Governor Clinton for one. They had a big wind fan there that cooled off the whole lobby, and Pepper strolled over in front of it with some sneezing powder folded into the crease of his newspaper. He opened the paper, and well . . . the whole lobby was cleaned out in two minutes. Bar and all.

—LEO DUROCHER
INFIELDER, 17 YEARS, 1925–1945;
MANAGER, 24 YEARS, 1939–1973;
WON THREE PENNANTS, ONE
WORLD SERIES; HALL OF FAME

I believe he could have continued to pitch shutouts until Christmas.

—GRANTLAND RICE
COLUMNIST, AUTHOR, 1900s–1950s,
AFTER MATHEWSON'S THIRD
SHUTOUT IN THE 1905 WORLD
SERIES

Be it recorded here,
New York possesses
the pitching marvel
of the century . . .

—*NEW YORK TIMES*, OCT. 15, 1905

I've only known three or four perfect swings in my time. This boy's got one of them.

—TY COBB
OUTFIELDER, 1905–1928; LIFETIME
BATTING AVERAGE .366; LED
LEAGUE IN HITTING 12 SEASONS;
892 STOLEN BASES; MANAGER,
1921–1926; HALL OF FAME

Always try for perfection. There's never been a perfect ball player. Willie Mays came closest. But always try.

—JOE DIMAGGIO

OUTFIELDER, 13 SEASONS, 1936–1948; .325 LIFETIME HITTER; HIT IN 56 CONSECUTIVE GAMES, 1941; HALL OF FAME

That Willie Mays, he's one of the greatest center fielders who ever lived. You can go back as far as you want and name all the great ones—Tris Speaker, Eddie Roush, Max Carey, Earl Combs, Joe DiMaggio. I don't care who you name, Mays is just as good, maybe better.

—HARRY HOOPER
**OUTFIELDER, 1909–1925;
HALL OF FAME**

Willie liked to extend his arms like Duke Snider, Mickey Mantle, and other power hitters, so if you crowded him with one pitch and then threw a pitch low and away you could give him trouble. Of course, you could pitch God that way, and it would give Him trouble.

—DON NEWCOMBE
PITCHER, TEN SEASONS, 1949–1960

Red Rolfe was originally a shortstop, too, but he didn't have the real good arm for making that long throw. I told him I was going to play him at third base.

"It's one of the easiest jobs in the infield," I told him. "You average about three chances a game. And don't worry about those hot smashes. That's a big joke. You've got a glove and you can stop them."

"Okay," he said.

He broke in at third up at Fenway Park. The first ball hit down to him took a bad bounce and hit him in the eye and blackened it. He came into the dugout holding his eye and said, "Joe, you gave me some bad information." But he became a good third baseman.

—JOE McCARTHY
MANAGER, 24 SEASONS, 1926–1950;
WON NINE PENNANTS, SEVEN
WORLD SERIES; HALL OF FAME

Looking out at the wavering farmhouse lights, ones which rushed through the darkened landscape, McCarthy had paused and said, "You know, Case [Stengel], that's the life for me. Nothing to worry about except get up and do the milking. Sometimes I think I'm in the greatest business in the world. Then you lose four straight and want to change places with the farmer."

—CURT SMITH
SPORTSWRITER, BASEBALL
BIOGRAPHER

Listen, any manager who can't get along with a .400 hitter ought to have his head examined.

—JOE McCARTHY

MANAGER, 24 SEASONS, 1926–1950; WON NINE PENNANTS, SEVEN WORLD SERIES; HALL OF FAME, ON BECOMING TED WILLIAMS'S MANAGER

The Cleveland Indians' great fastballer, Sudden Sam McDowell, would start complaining even before he released his pitch. "Ball?" he'd screech, then release it—"How can that be a ball?"

—RON LUCIANO
UMPIRE, 1968–1980; AUTHOR

If you made a bad play he'd say, "Son, come over here and sit down by me." You'd do that and he would say, "Now, why did you make that play that way?" Usually the fellow would say, "I thought—" and McGraw would interrupt and say, "With what? You just do the playing. I'll do the thinking for this club."

—BURLEIGH GRIMES
PITCHER, 1916–1934; 270 LIFETIME
WINS; MANAGER, 1937–1938;
HALL OF FAME

He combined the endearing personal traits of George Steinbrenner and Billy Martin—he was arrogant, combative, aggressive, insolent, cocksure, skillful, quick to take advantage, quick to take offense—and, like Steinbrenner and Martin, he was successful, a winner or close to it year after year.

—ROBERT W. CREAMER
SPORTSWRITER, BIOGRAPHER, EDITOR

The great majority of bats are supplied to major-league batters by Rawlings, Louisville Slugger, Hoosier, and, in the case of Mark McGwire, the NASA Jet Propulsion Laboratory.

—TIM McCARVER
CATCHER, 1959–1980;
SPORTSCASTER; SPORTSWRITER

He didn't learn to say hello until it was time to say goodbye.

—FRANK GRAHAM
SPORTSWRITER,
ON MEUSEL'S AFFABILITY DURING
HIS FINAL SEASON, AFTER YEARS
OF SURLINESS TO SPORTSWRITERS

When I was young I would listen to my subconscious, and my subconscious would always tell me what the pitcher was trying to do.

—STAN MUSIAL
OUTFIELDER, INFIELDER, 22
SEASONS. 1941-1963: .331 LIFETIME
BATTING AVERAGE, 475 HOME
RUNS: HALL OF FAME

Before Willie Mays's first appearance against the Cardinals, Leo Durocher ran down the St. Louis batting order for him, telling the rookie how the various batters should be played. He described the lead-off batter, and the number two man, and then moved to the clean-up hitter.

Mays interrupted to ask about number three.

"The third hitter," Durocher said, "is Stan Musial. There is no advice I can give you about him."

—DANIEL OKRENT AND STEVE WULF
SPORTSWRITERS

Commissioner of Baseball Kenesaw M. Landis once tried to explain to Newsom why he wanted him to stop playing the horses. "Damn it, Newsom," the Judge said, "a ballplayer who bets the horses can't keep his mind on baseball. Suppose you're pitching in a tight game and you have to bat in the ninth inning at just about the same time a horse you have a big bet on is running at the track. What will you be thinking of, the ball game or your bet?"

To which Newsom replied, "Mr. Commissioner, you don't have to worry about a thing. If it's a tight ball game in the ninth inning, they sure as hell won't have ol' Bobo up there hittin'."

—ROBERT W. CREAMER
SPORTSWRITER, BIOGRAPHER,
EDITOR

Mr. Kojiru Suzuki threw a sinker on the outside part of the plate. I followed the ball perfectly. I could almost feel myself waiting for its precise break before I let myself come forward. When I made contact, I felt like I was scooping the ball outward and upward. The ball rose slowly and steadily in the night sky, lit by Korakuen's bright lights. I could follow it all the way as it lazily reached its height and seemed to linger there in the haze, and then slowly began its descent into the right-field stands.

—SADAHARU OH
JAPANESE BASEBALL STAR; HIT 858
HOME RUNS

Ott is a standout with me. Ott is the
best-looking young player at the bat,
in my time with the club.

—JOHN McGRAW
INFIELDER, 1891–1906; .344
LIFETIME BATTING AVERAGE;
MANAGER, 33 YEARS, 1899–1932;
WON TEN PENNANTS, THREE
WORLD SERIES; HALL OF FAME

He had one of the great left arms,
he had the guts of a burglar and
for emergencies he kept a supply
of graphite oil on the inner side
of his belt.

—RED SMITH
COLUMNIST

Satch didn't get into the majors by throwin' the ball over the plate. He made it by throwin' it over a matchbook in the center of the plate.

—COOL PAPA BELL
LONGTIME STAR OUTFIELDER OF
NEGRO LEAGUES, HALL OF FAME

He would throw the ball on the corner just far enough so if you would swing, you couldn't get all the way around on it. Control. What you don't see in the big leagues now.

—JUDY JOHNSON
STAR INFIELDER OF NEGRO
LEAGUES: HALL OF FAME

It's like I said at Satchel [Paige]'s funeral in 1982: people say it's a shame he never pitched against the best. But who's to say he didn't?

—BUCK O'NEIL

STAR PLAYER, MANAGER IN NEGRO LEAGUES; COACH; SCOUT

Once, seeing Palmer reading *Dr. Zhivago*, teammate Steve Stone said, "It must be about an elbow specialist."

—THOMAS BOSWELL

SPORTSWRITER

I don't take one thing away from him for winning three hundred with the spitter. There are loopholes in the rules and you get away with what you can.

—DON BAYLOR
OUTFIELDER, 1970–1988: MANAGER,
1993–1998, 2000: COACH

Call me Liberace.

—DUSTY RHODES
OUTFIELDER, SEVEN SEASONS.
1952–1959, SEPTEMBER. 1954,
UPON RETURNING TO THE GIANTS'
BENCH AFTER STRIKING OUT,
HAVING DECLARED THAT HE WAS
GOING TO GET A HIT OFF THE
BROOKLYN DODGER'S ROOKIE
PITCHER KARL SPOONER "OR I'LL
KISS YOUR ASS"

Hey, George, flip me one
of them hanging curves.

—DUSTY RHODES

**OUTFIELDER, SEVEN SEASONS,
1952–1959,**

TO GEORGE SPENCER DURING
BATTING PRACTICE

He don't smoke, he don't drink, and he still can't hit .250.

—CASEY STENGEL
OUTFIELDER, 1912–1925; MANAGER, 1934–1943, 1949–1960, 1962–1965; WON TEN PENNANTS, SEVEN WORLD SERIES, FIVE IN A ROW; COACH; HALL OF FAME

"Cal Ripken," [Orioles General Manager Roland] Hemond said, "plays the infield like a manager." By this he meant that Ripken is a cerebral player, constantly moving in response to the changed situation, from pitch to pitch, in anticipation of what his pitcher will do, which depends on what the pitcher expects the batter to expect (which depends on what the batter thinks the pitcher expects him to expect).

—GEORGE F. WILL
COLUMNIST

I had a fine right arm and a great delivery, but I pitched too much and wore myself down. I wasn't quite selfish enough or smart enough.

—ROBIN ROBERTS
PITCHER, 1948–1966; WON 245 GAMES; HALL OF FAME

Make it rain, Brooksie.

—FELLOW ORIOLE PLAYER AFTER
ANOTHER SPECTACULAR PLAY AT
THIRD BASE DURING THE 1970
WORLD SERIES

He belongs in a higher league.

—PETE ROSE

INFIELDER, OUTFIELDER, 1963–1986;
SET LIFETIME RECORDS OF 3,562
MAJOR LEAGUE GAMES PLAYED,
14,053 TIMES AT BAT, 4,256 BASE
HITS; MANAGER, 1984–1986;
BANNED FROM BASEBALL IN
1989 FOR GAMBLING,

DURING 1970 WORLD SERIES

I know 91 pitchers and 9 managers
in the league who will chip in $500
apiece if [Frank] Robinson will go
through on his plans to retire. That's
$50,000 for him.

—GENE MAUCH
INFIELDER, NINE SEASONS,
1944–1957; MANAGER, 1960–1982,
1985-87

Mr. Rickey, I've got to do it.

—JACKIE ROBINSON
INFIELDER, 1947–1956; .311 LIFETIME
BATTING AVERAGE; IN 1947 BECAME
THE FIRST BLACK PLAYER IN
MAJOR LEAGUES; HALL OF FAME.
WHEN ASKED BY BRANCH RICKEY
WHETHER HE COULD TAKE THE
ABUSE HE WOULD RECEIVE UPON
BEING THE FIRST BLACK PLAYER IN
THE MAJOR LEAGUES, WITHOUT
FIGHTING BACK

We didn't think he was the best. He ran well and he was a fighter, but he wasn't one of the Negro "stars." It just goes to show you that you can't always tell about a ballplayer. Branch Rickey saw something there and he was right. Robinson was the man for the job, college-educated, a winner, a man with good self-control.

—BUCK LEONARD
STAR INFIELDER IN NEGRO
LEAGUES, 1933–1950;
HALL OF FAME

You saw how he stood there at the plate and dared them to hit him with the ball and you began to put yourself in his shoes. You'd think of yourself trying to break in the black leagues maybe, and what it would be like—and I know that I couldn't have done it. In a word: he was winning respect.

—PEE WEE REESE
INFIELDER, 16 SEASONS, 1940–1958;
HALL OF FAME

Why don't you guys go to work on somebody who can fight back? There isn't one of you has the guts of a louse.

—EDDIE STANKY
INFIELDER, 1943–1953; MANAGER.
1952–1955, 1966–1968. 1977; COACH.
**TO PHILADELPHIA PHILLIES RIDING
JACKIE ROBINSON IN 1947**

They ought to put some of those [black] guys in the Hall of Fame, I told Casey Stengel, "The guys they put in the Hall of Fame are a joke. [Bullet Joe] Rogan's the guy ought to go in." Casey recommended it to the commissioner, but it never took.

—BABE HERMAN
OUTFIELDER, 1926-1937, 1945

Everyone seemed to love Pete the player: the fans, the writers, the umpires, the managers, the ground crew, everyone associated with the game. We respected him so much that we sometimes forgot to assess his playing skills adequately. No one ever said that about Cobb. No one said that Cobb was the kind of guy they would have enjoyed playing with, that he brought out the best in you. No one ever said that they respected Cobb so much that they forgot how good he was.

—CRAIG R. WRIGHT
SPORTSWRITER; BASEBALL STATISTICIAN

I don't think Pete Rose deserves to be in the Hall of Fame because he was offered a chance to come clean, and he didn't come clean. He has never really admitted that he did something wrong. He has never really come right out and said, "Yes, I'm guilty [of betting on baseball games in which he played and managed]. And I'm just sorry for the whole thing."

—MONTE IRVIN
STAR IN NEGRO LEAGUES;
INFIELDER, OUTFIELDER, 1949–1956;
HALL OF FAME

But the key moment in the Yankees '51 campaign came in a critical September game against Cleveland at Yankee Stadium before a crowd of 68,000, with the score tied in the ninth, DiMaggio on third, and Phil Rizzuto, then the game's most accomplished bunter, at the plate. The combination of Rizzuto's special talent and DiMaggio's skill as a runner made the game-winning squeeze play foreordained. "Tell me," DiMaggio said idly to Al Rosen, the Cleveland third baseman. "Do you think he's going to bunt?" "I'll be the most surprised Jew in the place if he doesn't," Rosen responded. In the outcome, Rosen was not surprised.

—CHARLES EINSTEIN
SPORTSWRITER

A theory had been advanced that because Ruth was such a pronounced pull hitter, he could be stopped if he were given nothing but low outside pitches. Chicago's Eddie Cicotte tested the theory and Ruth hit three successive doubles to the opposite field. The next day he hit another double and two triples. End of theory.

—ROBERT W. CREAMER
SPORTSWRITER, BIOGRAPHER,
EDITOR

Not many pitchers I interviewed had trouble with Ruth, because they kept the ball low and away from him. It makes one wonder off of whom he hit those 714 home runs?

—EUGENE MURDOCK
BASEBALL HISTORIAN

He had a heap of living
to do to make up for the
grim years of his youth.
And he never thought
there would be an end
to his skills.

—CLAIRE MERRITT HODGSON RUTH

BABE RUTH'S SECOND WIFE

I knew Ruth couldn't hit with me—that is, real batting—or run bases with me—or (play) outfield with me.

—TY COBB
OUTFIELDER, 1905–1928; LIFETIME
BATTING AVERAGE .366; LED
LEAGUE IN HITTING 12 SEASONS;
892 STOLEN BASES, MANAGER,
1921–1926; HALL OF FAME

Because of Ruth's bulk, [Jacob] Ruppert decided to dress the Yankees in the now-traditional pinstripe uniform and dark blue stockings. The natty, clothes-conscious Ruppert felt the new uniform would make Babe look trimmer. The Yankees also introduced uniform numbers to the major leagues in 1929. Ruth's number was number 3 because he batted third, Gehrig's 4 because he batted fourth, and so on.

—ROBERT W. CREAMER
SPORTSWRITER, BIOGRAPHER, EDITOR

You know, I saw it all happen, from beginning to end. But sometimes I still can't believe what I saw: this nineteen-year-old kid, crude, poorly educated, only lightly brushed by the social veneer we call civilization, gradually transformed into the idol of American youth and the symbol of baseball the world over—a man loved by more people and with an intensity of feeling that perhaps has never been equaled before or since. I saw a man transformed from a human being into something pretty close to a god.

—HARRY HOOPER
OUTFIELDER, 1909–1925;
HALL OF FAME

He was easy to like and was at his best in the clutch. To me he was the most exciting player to watch of all time.

—BILL DICKEY
CATCHER, 1928–1946; LIFETIME
.313 HITTER; MANAGER, 1946;
HALL OF FAME

There are a lot of people who would rather watch Babe Ruth hit a long fly than see Hack Wilson smack the ball over the garden wall. One is an artist, the other a plumber.

—JOE WILLIAMS
COLUMNIST, 1910s–1950s

Ruth was calming down rapidly [after invading the Giants' clubhouse], and when one of McGraw's coaches told him he'd better leave he said, "All right. I know I shouldn't have come in here, but I wanted to get things straight. Listen, I'm sorry, fellows. Tomorrow, let's cut out the rough stuff and just play baseball."

Heinie Groh, the Giants' third baseman, hooted. The day before, Ruth had slid into Groh like a fullback hitting the line. "Baseball?" said Groh. "Look who's talking. Yesterday I thought we were playing football."

Everybody laughed. Ruth and [Bob] Meusel started to go, but at the door Babe turned back for a moment. "Don't get me wrong, fellows," he said seriously. "I don't mind being called a prick or a cocksucker or things like that. I expect that. But lay off the personal stuff."

—ROBERT W. CREAMER
SPORTSWRITER, BIOGRAPHER,
EDITOR

I was looking for a fast-ball, he threw a curve and I got vapor-locked.

—BRAD MILLS

INFIELDER, 1980–1983,

AFTER BECOMING NOLAN RYAN'S
4,000TH STRIKEOUT VICTIM

During a game, Schmidt brings such formidable attention and intelligence to bear on the enemy pitcher that one senses that the odds have almost been reversed out there: it is the man on the mound, not the one up at the plate, who is in worse trouble from the start.

—ROGER ANGELL
AUTHOR, EDITOR

I learned to let my talent dictate what I was on a given day. I learned to adjust to it, its limits, to what it told me about myself. I couldn't do more than I was physically or mentally capable of. If I tried to throw harder than I could, the ball went slower than it normally would.

—TOM SEAVER
PITCHER, 1967–1986; 311 LIFETIME
VICTORIES; HALL OF FAME

For that one year (1922) at least he must have been the most remarkable ball player we ever saw . . .

—ALLISON DANZIG
SPORTSWRITER, AUTHOR

Ozzie Smith just made another play that I've never seen anyone else make before, and I've seen him make it more than anyone else ever has.

—JERRY COLEMAN
INFIELDER, 1949–1957; MANAGER, 1980; SPORTSCASTER

THERE MAY BE SLIGHT
DELAYS WHEN SAMMY
SOSA'S AT BAT.

—CHICAGO TRANSIT AUTHORITY
SIGN NEAR ELEVATED TRAIN STOP
AT WRIGLEY FIELD, 1998

Bezball been berry, berry good to me!

—SAMMY SOSA

OUTFIELDER, 1989– ; HIT 66 HOME RUNS IN 1998

I don't think Spahn will ever get
into the Hall of Fame. He'll never
stop pitching.

—STAN MUSIAL
OUTFIELDER, INFIELDER, 22
SEASONS, 1941–1963; .331 LIFETIME
BATTING AVERAGE, 475 HOME
RUNS; HALL OF FAME

He simply did everything well. I don't think you could ask for a better all-around ball player.

—SMOKY JOE WOOD
PITCHER, OUTFIELDER, 14 YEARS.
1909–1922

Only once did Stallings forget the name of a car owned by one of his players. Seeking to call attention to the mental shortcomings of [Hank] Gowdy, who missed a sign one day, the Braves' manager turned to the rest of the bench.

"Look at him up there," he spattered derisively, "the—the—" And there was a pause as Stallings tried in vain to recall the name of the car driven by Gowdy. He was stumped, but not for long.

"Look at him," yelled Stallings, "the bicycle-riding so-and-so."

—TOM MEANY
SPORTSWRITER, 1920s–1950s

He can't run, he can't hit and he can't throw. But if there's a way to beat the other team, he'll find it.

—BRANCH RICKEY
CATCHER, 1905–1907, 1914;
MANAGER, TEN SEASONS,
1913–1925; EXECUTIVE, 1910s–1950s;
PIONEERED IN FARM SYSTEM;
ENDED RACIAL SEGREGATION
IN PROFESSIONAL BASEBALL;
HALL OF FAME

I think if you have a leader like a Willie Stargell on your team you're all right.

—ROBIN ROBERTS
PITCHER, 1948–1966; WON 245
GAMES; HALL OF FAME

He could make a sick
monkey laugh.

—BOB SMITH

PITCHER, 1923–1937

A few days later when he failed to slide and was tagged out, the crowd hooted as he returned to the dugout. There weren't many people in the stands, and it wasn't hard to hear him when he paused before going into the dugout, looked up at the crowd, and said, "With the salary I get I'm so hollow and starving that if I slide I'm liable to explode like a light bulb."

—ROBERT W. CREAMER
SPORTSWRITER, BIOGRAPHER, EDITOR

The paths of glory lead but to the Braves.

—CASEY STENGEL

OUTFIELDER, 1912–1925; MANAGER,
1934–1943, 1949–1960. 1962–1965;
WON TEN PENNANTS. SEVEN
WORLD SERIES. FIVE IN A ROW;
COACH; HALL OF FAME,

UPON BEING TRADED TO THE
BOSTON BRAVES AFTER HIS
OUTSTANDING 1923 WORLD SERIES
FOR THE NEW YORK GIANTS

Casey Stengel is said to have watched a long drive to center go past his center fielder, and bounce around behind the three monuments [in Yankee Stadium] while his outfielder had troubles picking it up. Finally, Casey yelled, "Ruth, Gehrig, Huggins—somebody throw the ball."

—PHILIP J. LOWRY
BASEBALL HISTORIAN

"You are retiring of your own volition, aren't you, Mr. Stengel?" asked [Dan] Topping. There was a moment of silence in which you could have heard a pin drop. Then Stengel, raising his voice, electrified the session by saying crisply, "Boys, I'm not retiring; I've just been fired." On this low note ended Stengel's magnificent career with the Yankees.

—FRED LIEB
SPORTSWRITER

I got this broken arm from watching my team. We're improving magnificently. All they gave me last year was a head cold.

—CASEY STENGEL
ON THE NEW YORK METS

That [World Series] ring don't cost so much. I got four or five rings and don't know whether I'm going to wear five of them when I go out. Unless you're broke, the ring is the best thing you can get which money comes in handy all the time. If a player don't shoot he can go and play against us which is all right in the first place too. The situation is for five years and they still haven't found the end of it, the other guys. They say the owners are rich, so what? We must have the umpires, not the same ones. It's the money the Yankees got. On the ball club you can't write it all down. You do it. So they say it's the lively ball and the damn bunting. . . . What about the shortstop Rizzuto who got nothing but daughters but throws out the left-handed hitters in the double play?

—CASEY STENGEL

Everybody knows that Casey [Stengel] has forgotten more baseball than I'll ever know. That's the trouble, he's forgotten it.

—JIMMY PIERSALL
OUTFIELDER, 17 SEASONS,
1950–1967

I'm in the twilight of a mediocre career.

—FRANK SULLIVAN
PITCHER, 1953–1963

I ought to get a Black
and Decker commercial
out of it.

—DON SUTTON
**PITCHER, 1966–1988; 324 LIFETIME
WINS; SPORTSCASTER;
HALL OF FAME,**
ON HIS REPUTATION FOR SCUFFING
UP BASEBALLS

It was unbelievable. I had just been trying to make contact. But I'll be darned if it didn't go out. I started around the bases and when I was turning second base I thought I'd look for my folks in the crowd. I knew about where they were sitting, in the third-base boxes. Sure enough, there was my father, jumping up and down and applauding and yelling. With it being a Cincinnati crowd there weren't too many people doing that, and I guess that's how I was able to spot him. I caught his eye and for those few seconds we were looking at each other. It was a great feeling.

—GENE TENACE
CATCHER, 1969–1983; COACH

The son of a bitch was some
kind of hitter.

—TED WILLIAMS
OUTFIELDER, 19 YEARS, 1939–1960;
.344 LIFETIME BATTING AVERAGE,
521 HOMERS; MANAGER, 1969–1972;
HIT .406 IN 1941; HALL OF FAME

It was the most famous home run ever made. He hit it in 3,000,000 living rooms, to say nothing of the bars and grills.

—GARRY SCHUMACHER
SPORTSWRITER, PUBLICIST,
ON BOBBY THOMSON'S PENNANT-
WINNING HOME RUN FOR THE
GIANTS IN 1951

If Bob Uecker had not been on the Cardinals, then it's questionable whether we could have beaten the Yankees [in 1964]. He kept everything so funny that we never had the chance to think of what a monumental event we were playing in, against the New York Yankees of all teams.

—TIM McCARVER
CATCHER, 1959–1980;
SPORTSCASTER; SPORTSWRITER

He had more stuff than any pitcher I ever saw. He had everything but a sense of responsibility.

—CONNIE MACK
CATCHER, 1886–1896; MANAGER, 53
SEASONS, 1894–1950; WON EIGHT
PENNANTS, FIVE WORLD SERIES;
HALL OF FAME

Nobody ever saw anything graceful or picturesque about Wagner on the diamond. His movements have been likened to the gambols of a caracoling elephant. He is ungainly and so bow-legged that when he runs his limbs seem to be moving in a circle after the fashion of a propeller. But he can run like the wind.

—*NEW YORK AMERICAN*, NOV. 19, 1907

One day he was batting against a young pitcher who had just come into the league. The catcher was a kid, too. A rookie battery. The pitcher threw Honus a curveball, and he swung at it and missed and fell down on one knee. Looked helpless as a robin. I was kind of surprised, but the guy sitting next to me on the bench poked me in the ribs and said, "Watch this next one." Those kids figured they had the old man's weaknesses, you see, and served him up the same dish—as he knew they would. Well, Honus hit a line drive so hard the fence in left field went back and forth for five minutes.

—BURLEIGH GRIMES
PITCHER, 1916–1934; 270 LIFETIME
WINS; MANAGER, 1937–1938; HALL
OF FAME

We'd be lounging in the Astro bullpen and Harry would call down to tell us to be alert so we could holler to our right fielder which base to throw to in the event he had to turn his back to get a ball off the wall. An important detail that could mean the ball game and only Harry Walker would think of it. Then we'd spend the rest of the game griping about what a pain Harry Walker was to interfere with our leisure time.

—JIM BOUTON
PITCHER, 1962–1970, 1978; AUTHOR

He had to be a very graceful
player, because he could slide
without breaking the bottle
on his hip.

—CASEY STENGEL
OUTFIELDER. 1912–1925; MANAGER,
1934–1943, 1949–1960, 1962–1965;
WON TEN PENNANTS. SEVEN
WORLD SERIES. FIVE IN A ROW;
COACH; HALL OF FAME

[Charles Dryden described] Ed Walsh of the White Sox as the "only man in the world who can strut sitting down."

—JONATHAN YARDLEY
AUTHOR, BOOK CRITIC

I think catching Hoyt Wilhelm and his knucklers ruined my career. The more I caught him, the worse I got.

—GUS TRIANDOS
CATCHER, 1953–1965

All I want out of life is that when I walk down the street folks will say, "There goes the greatest hitter that ever lived."

—TED WILLIAMS
OUTFIELDER, 19 YEARS, 1939–1960;
.344 LIFETIME BATTING AVERAGE,
521 HOMERS; MANAGER, 1969–1972;
HIT .406 IN 1941; HALL OF FAME,
AS A YOUNG PLAYER

One of the remarkable things about him is that he never goes after a bad ball. He must have a wonderful pair of eyes. What's his weakness? I don't think he has anything approaching a weakness.

—JIMMY FOXX
INFIELDER, CATCHER, 1925–1945; 534
LIFETIME HOME RUNS, .325 BATTING
AVERAGE; HALL OF FAME

If ever a player deserved to hit .400, it's Ted. He never sat down against tough pitchers. He never bunted. He didn't have the advantage of the sacrifice-fly rule like those hitters before him.

—JOE CRONIN
INFIELDER, 1926–1945; MANAGER
1933–1947; WON ONE PENNANT;
GENERAL MANAGER RED SOX,
1948–1959; PRESIDENT AMERICAN
LEAGUE, 1959–1973; HALL OF FAME,
AFTER WILLIAMS HAD HIT .406
IN 1941

If the average player was going to bat four times in a game and got hits his first three times up, he'd be satisfied even if he failed the fourth time up. He'd relax after the third hit. Ted was his most vicious his fourth time up. That's what set him apart.

—PUMPSIE GREEN
INFIELDER, 1959–1963

TED WILLIAMS

Every third word out of Williams's mouth was a swear word. These adjectives were an absolutely essential part of his baseball vocabulary. One night, in Washington, President Nixon used our locker room as his ballpark office . . .

After the game [Nixon] paused to talk baseball with us. I was my usual delightful self, being smart enough not to mention football, and was in the middle of a wonderful story about me when Williams rapped on the door.

The four umpires in the room became so quiet you could have heard a stolen baseball drop.

The Secret Service agents brought Williams into the room. I knew exactly what was coming and closed my eyes, although that did not affect my hearing. "Hey," Williams said after being introduced to the President of the United States. "How the $&#* are you?"

Nixon didn't hesitate. He looked at the four of us and said, "Oh, don't worry about that. I've met the $&#*#$ before."

—RON LUCIANO
UMPIRE, 1968–1980; AUTHOR

Best hitter I ever saw? No, not Cobb,
not Joe Jackson, not Babe Ruth.
Teddy Williams. No question. He
could do everything.

—JIMMY DYKES
**INFIELDER, 1918–1939; MANAGER,
21 SEASONS, 1934–1961**

My first two years, when Carl Yastrzemski was up, if Carl didn't swing, it was not a strike. And I mean to tell you I threw balls right down the middle of the plate, belt-high, and you could not doubt it, but if Carl didn't swing, it was not a strike.

—JACK MORRIS

1977–1994, 254 LIFETIME WINS

The record book shows that, at one time or another during his thirteen seasons of major league baseball, Rudy York was an outfielder, a third baseman, and a catcher as well as a third baseman. If this suggests the adjective "versatile," it is misleading. No matter where he was stationed in the field, Rudy York always played the same position.

He played bat.

—RED SMITH
COLUMNIST

A man who isn't willing to work
from dreary morn till weary eve
shouldn't think about becoming
a pitcher.

—CY YOUNG
PITCHER, 1890–1911; WON 511 GAMES;
PITCHED 7,356 INNINGS;
HALL OF FAME

SOURCES

Alexander, Charles C., *John McGraw*. New York: Viking Press, 1988.

Alexander, Charles C., *Our Game: An American Baseball History*. New York: Henry Holt, 1991.

Alexander, Charles C., *Rogers Hornsby: A Biography*. New York: Henry Holt and Co., 1995.

Allen, Lee, *Cooperstown Corner: Columns from The Sporting News, 1962–1969*. Cleveland, Ohio: Society for American Baseball Research, n.d.

Allen, Maury, *Baseball: The Lives behind the Seams*. New York: Macmillan Publishing Co., 1990.

Alvarez, Mark, "An Interview with Smoky Joe Wood," *Baseball Research Journal* [No. 16], 1987.

Angell, Roger, *Late Innings: A Baseball Companion*. New York: Simon and Schuster, 1982.

Angell, Roger, *Season Ticket: A Baseball Companion*. Boston: Houghton Mifflin, 1988.

Aschburner, Steve, "Beasts of Burden," *Street and Smith's Baseball* (March, 1999).

Bamberger, Michael, "Sammy: You're the Man," *Sports Illustrated*, 89, 13 (September 28, 1998).

Barber, Red, *The Rhubarb Patch: The Story of the Modern Brooklyn Dodgers*. New York: Simon and Schuster, 1954.

Barber, Red, *1947: When Hell Broke Loose in Baseball*. Garden City, N. Y.: Doubleday and Co., 1982.

Barber, Red, *Walk in the Spirit*. New York: The Dial Press, 1969.

Barber, Red, and Robert Creamer, *Rhubarb in the Catbird Seat*. Garden City, N. Y.: Doubleday and Co., 1968.

Baseball. Photographs by Walter Iooss, Jr. Text by Roger Angell. New York: Harry N. Abrams, 1984.

Bax, Richard, *Ty Cobb: His Tumultuous Life and Times*. Dallas, Tex.: Taylor Publishing Co., 1994.

Benchley, Robert, *Love Conquers All*. New York: Henry Holt and Co., 1922.

Bethel, Dell, *Inside Baseball: Tips and Techniques for Coaches and Players*. Chicago: Henry Regnery Co., 1969.

Boswell, Thomas, *How Life Imitates the World Series: An Inquiry into the Game*. Garden City, N.Y.: Doubleday and Co., 1982.

Boswell, Thomas, *Why Time Begins on Opening Day*. Garden City, N.Y.: Doubleday and Co., 1984.

Boswell, Thomas, *The Heart of the Order*. New York: Doubleday and Co., 1989.

Bouton, Jim, *Ball Four: plus Ball Five*. New York: Stein and Day, 1981. [*Ball Four* orig. publ. 1970]

Bouton, Jim, with Neil Offen, "*I Managed Good, But Boy Did They Play Bad*." Chicago: Playboy Press, 1973.

Bready, James H., *The Home Team: 1859–1959, A Full Century of Baseball in Baltimore*. n.p., [1959].

Broeg, Bob, *The Pilot Light and the Gas House Gang*. St. Louis, Mo.: The Bethany Press, 1980.

Brosnan, Jim, *The Long Season*. New York: Penguin Books, 1983. [originally publ. 1960].

Cairns, Bob, *Pen Men: Baseball's Greatest Bullpen Stories Told by the Men Who Brought the Game Relief*. New York: St. Martin's Press, 1992.

Callahan, Gerry, "A Fall Classic," *Sports Illustrated*, 87, 13 (September 29, 1997).

Church, Seymour R., *Base Ball: The History, Statistics and Romance of the American National Game*. Vol. I. The 1902 Edition in Facsimile. Introduction by Brock Brower. Princeton, N.J.: The Pine Press, 1974.

Cobb, Ty, with Al Stump, *My Life in Baseball: The True Record*. Introduction by Charles C. Alexander. Lincoln: University of Nebraska Press, 1993. [orig. publ. 1961].

Cochrane, Gordon S. (Mickey), *Baseball: The Fan's Game*. Cleveland, Ohio: Society for American Baseball Research, 1992. [orig. publ. 1939].

Connor, Anthony J., *Baseball for the Love of It: Hall of Famers Tell It Like It Was*. New York: Macmillan Publishing Co., 1982.

Creamer, Robert W., *Babe: The Legend Comes to Life*. New York: Simon and Schuster, 1974.

Creamer, Robert W., *Baseball in '41: A Celebration of the "Best Baseball Season Ever"—in the Year America Went to War*. New York: Penguin Books, 1992.

Creamer, Robert W., *Mantle Remembered*. New York: Warner Books, 1995.

Creamer, Robert W., *Stengel: His Life and Times*. New York: Simon and Schuster, 1984.

Crowther, Hal, *Unarmed but Dangerous: Withering Attacks on All Things Phoney, Foolish, and Fundamentally Wrong with America Today*. Atlanta, Ga.: Longstreet Press, 1995.

Danzig, Allison, and Joe Reichler, *The History of Baseball: Its Great Players, Teams and Managers*. Englewood Cliffs, N.J.: Prentice-Hall, 1959.

Dittmar, Joe, "Tim Hurst," *The National Pastime*. No. 17 (1997).

Durocher, Leo, with Ed Linn, *Nice Guys Finish Last*. New York: Simon and Schuster, 1973.

Egenreither, Richard, "Chris Von der Ahe: Baseball's Pioneering Huckster," *Baseball Research Journal*, No. 18 (1989).

Einstein, Charles, *Willie's Time: A Memoir*. New York: Berkley Books, 1979.

Farrell, James T., *My Baseball Diary*. New York: A. S. Barnes and Co., 1957.

Falkner, David, *The Short Season: The Hard Work and High Times of Baseball in the Spring*. New York: Times Books, 1986.

Feinstein, John, *Play Ball: The Life and Troubled Times of Major League Baseball*. New York: Villard, 1993.

Feldman, Jay, "Tweed Webb: He's Seen 'Em All," *Baseball Research Journal*, No. 18 (1989).

Fleming, G. H., *The Unforgettable Season*. Foreword by Lawrence Ritter. New York: Simon and Schuster, 1981.

Frommer, Harvey, *Baseball's Greatest Managers*. New York: Franklin Watts, 1985.

Frommer, Harvey, *Shoeless Joe and Ragtime Baseball*. Dallas, Tex.: Taylor Publishing Co., 1992.

Giamatti, A. Bartlett, *A Great and Glorious Game: Baseball Writings of A. Bartlett Giamatti*, edited by Kenneth S. Robson. Foreword by David Halberstam. Chapel Hill, N.C.: Algonquin Books of Chapel Hill, 1998.

Gmelch, George, and J. J. Winer, *In the Ballpark: The Working Lives of Baseball People*. Washington, D.C.: Smithsonian Institution Press, 1998.

Graham, Frank, *The New York Giants: An Informal History*. New York: G. P. Putnam's Sons, 1952.

Grayson, Harry, "Honus Wagner," NEA feature story, 1943.

Grossinger, Richard, and Kevin Kerrane, ed., *Into the Temple of Baseball*. Berkeley, Calif.: Celestial Arts, 1990.

Gutman, Dan, *Baseball Babylon: From the Black Sox to Pete Rose, the Real Stories behind the Scandals that Rocked the Game*. New York: Penguin Books, 1992.

Hall, Donald, *Fathers Playing Catch with Sons: Essays on Sports* [Mostly Baseball]. San Francisco: North Point Press, 1985.

Holtzman, Jerome, ed., *No Cheering in the Press Box*. Rev. and expanded ed. New York: Henry Holt, 1995.

Holway, John B., *Blackball Stars: Negro League Pioneers*. Westport, Ct.: Meckler Books, 1988.

Holway, John B., *Josh and Satch: The Life and Times of Josh Gibson and Satchel Paige*. New York: Carroll and Graf Publishers/Richard Gallen, 1992.

Honig, Donald, *Baseball When the Grass Was Real: Baseball from the Twenties to the Forties Told by the Men Who Played It*. New York: Coward, McCann & Geoghegan, 1975.

Honig, Donald, *The Man in the Dugout: Fifteen Big League Managers Speak Their Minds*. Chicago, Ill.: Follett Publishing Company, 1977.

Honig, Donald, *The October Heroes: Great World Series Games Remembered by the Men Who Played Them*. New York: Simon & Schuster, 1979.

Irvin, Monte, with James A. Riley, *Nice Guys Finish First*. New York: Carroll and Graf, 1996.

Johnson, Dick, "A Conversation with Roger Angell," *SABR Review of Books*, III (1988).

Jordan, Pat, *The Suitors of Spring*. New York: Warner Paperback Library, 1974.

Kachline, Clifford, "Big Individual Performances Highlight Exciting '86 Season." *Official Baseball Guide*: 1987 Edition. St. Louis, Mo.: *The Sporting News*, 1988.

Kahn, Roger, *A Season in the Sun*. New York: Harper and Row, 1977.

Kahn, Roger, *The Boys of Summer*. New York: New American Library, 1973. [orig. publ. 1971].

Kaplan, Evan, "A Season to Remember," *Street and Smith's Baseball* (March, 1999).

Kaplan, Jim, *Pine-Tarred and Feathered: A Year on the Baseball Beat*. Chapel Hill, N.C.: Algonquin Books of Chapel Hill, 1985.

Kaplan, Jim, *Playing the Field*. Chapel Hill, N.C.: Algonquin Books of Chapel Hill, 1987.

Kerrane, Kevin, *Dollar Sign on the Muscle: The World of Baseball Scouting*. New York: Beaufort Books, 1984.

Kiersch, Edward, *Where Have You Gone, Vince DiMaggio?* New York: Bantam Books, 1983.

Kilgallen, James L., "Looking 'Em Over: New York Yankees," *International News Service*, 1939.

Koppett, Leonard, *All About Baseball*. New York: Quadrangle / New York Times Book Co., 1974.

Lardner, Ring W., *Some Champions: Sketches and Fiction*. ed. Matthew J. Bruccoli and Richard Layman. New York: Charles Scribner's Sons, 1976.

Lardner, Ring, W. *You Know Me Al: A Busher's Letters*. New York: Charles Scribner's Sons, 1960. (originally published 1916).

Lehmann-Haupt, Christopher, *Me and DiMaggio: A Baseball Fan Goes in Search of His Gods*. New York: Simon and Schuster, 1986.

Lieb, Fred, *Baseball As I Have Known It*. Foreword by Larry Ritter. New York: Coward, McCann and Geoghehan, 1977.

Lowry, Philip J., *Green Cathedrals*. Preface by Philip H. Bess. Cooperstown, N. Y.: Society for American Baseball Research, 1986.

Luciano, Ron, and David Fisher, *The Umpire Strikes Back*. Toronto and New York: Bantam Books, 1982.

Luciano, Ron, and David Fisher, *Remembrance of Swings Past*. New York: Bantam Books, 1988.

Lyle, Sparky, with Peter Golenbock, *The Bronx Zoo*. New York: Crown Books, 1979.

Maranville, Walter "Rabbit," *Run, Rabbit, Run: The Hilarious and Mostly True Tales of Rabbit Maranville*. Cleveland, Ohio: Society for American Baseball Research, 1991.

Marazzi, Rich, *The Rules and Lore of Baseball*. New York: Stein and Day, 1980.

Mathewson, Christy, *Pitching In a Pinch*. Introduction by Red Smith. New York: Stein and Day, 1977. [orig. publ. 1912, written by Jack Wheeler].

McCarver, Tim, with Danny Peary, *Tim McCarver's Baseball for Brain Surgeons and Other Fans: Understanding and Interpreting the Game So You Can Watch It like a Pro*. New York: Villard, 1998.

Murdock, Eugene, *Baseball Between the Wars: Memories of the Game by the Men Who Played It*. Westport, Ct.: Meckler Publishing, 1992.

Murdock, Eugene, *Baseball Players and Their Times: Oral Histories of the Game, 1920–1940*. Westport, Ct.: Meckler Publishing, 1991.

Murphy, J. M., *Napoleon Lajoie: Modern Baseball's First Superstar. The National Pastime: A Review of Baseball History*, Vol. VII, No. 1 (spring, 1988).

Nash, Bruce, and Allan Zullo, *The Baseball Hall of Shame, 2*. Bernie Ward, Curator. New York: Pocket Books, 1986.

Nemec, David, *The Rules of Baseball: An Anecdotal Look at the Rules of Baseball and How They Came To Be*. New York: The Lyons Press, 1994.

Nemec, Raymond J., "The Performance and Personality of Percy Werden," *Baseball Research Journal*, 1977.

Okrent, Daniel, and Steve Wulf, *Baseball Anecdotes*. New York: Oxford University Press, 1989.

O'Neil, Buck, with Steve Wulf and David Conrads, *I Was Right on Time*. New York: Simon & Schuster, 1996.

Pascarelli, Peter, *The Toughest Job in Baseball: What Managers Do, How They Do It, and Why It Gives Them Ulcers*. New York: Simon and Schuster, 1993.

Peary, Daniel, ed., *We Played the Game: 65 Players Remember Baseball's Greatest Era, 1947–1964*. New York: Hyperion Books, 1996.

Polner, Murray, *Branch Rickey: A Biography*. New York: Atheneum, 1982.

Quigley, Martin, *The Crooked Pitch: The Curveball in American Baseball History*. Chapel Hill, N.C.: Algonquin Books of Chapel Hill, 1984.

Ritter, Lawrence S., *The Glory of Their Times: The Story of the Early Days of Baseball Told by the Men Who Played It*. New and enlarged ed. New York: William Morrow and Co., 1984.

Robinson, Ray, *Matty—An American Hero: Christopher Mathewson of the New York Giants*. New York: Oxford University Press, 1993.

Ruth, George Herman, *Babe Ruth's Own Book of Baseball*. Bison Books Introduction by Jerome Holtzman. Lincoln: Univ. of Nebraska Press, 1992. [orig. publ. 1928; written by Ford C. Frick].

Ryan, Nolan, with Mickey Herskovitz, *Kings of the Hill: An Irreverent Look at the Men on the Mound*. New York: HarperCollins, 1992.

Selzer, Jack, *Baseball in the Nineteenth Century: An Overview*. Cooperstown, N.Y.: Society for American Baseball Research, 1986.

Smart, Steve, "Les Tietje," *The National Pastime: A Review of Baseball History*, No. 13 (1993).

Smelser, Marshall, *The Life That Ruth Built*. New York: Quadrangle / The New York Times Books, 1975.

Smith, Curt, *America's Dizzy Dean*. St. Louis, Mo.: The Bethany Press, 1978.

Smith, Red, *Press Box: Red Smith's Favorite Sports Stories*. New York: W. W. Norton, 1974.

Smith, Red, *To Absent Friends from Red Smith*. New York: Atheneum Publishers, 1982.

Solomon, Burt, *Where They Ain't: The Fabled Life and Untimely Death of the Original Baltimore Orioles, the Team that Gave Birth to Modern Baseball*. New York: The Free Press, 1999.

Spalding's Official Baseball Guide, 1937.

Spalding-Reach Official Base Ball Guide, 1941.

Stein, Fred, *Under Coogan's Bluff: A Fan's Recollections of the New York Giants under Terry and Ott*. Glenshaw, Pa.: Chapter and Cask, 1981.

Stout, Glenn, "Where Baseball Literature Begins," *SABR Review of Books*, III (1988).

Stump, Al, *Cobb: A Biography*. Chapel Hill, N.C.: Algonquin Books of Chapel Hill, 1994.

Sullivan, Dean A., ed., *Middle Innings: A Documentary History of Baseball, 1900–1948*. Lincoln: University of Nebraska Press, 1998.

Thorn, John, ed., *The Armchair Book of Baseball*. New York: Charles Scribner's Sons, 1985.

Thorn, John, Pete Palmer, Michael Gershman, David Pietrusza, and Dan Schlossberg, *Total Braves*. New York: Penguin Books, 1996.

Thorn, John, and Pete Palmer, *Total Baseball*. 2nd Edition. New York: Warner Books, 1991.

Thorn, John, Pete Palmer, Michael Gershman, and David Pietrusza, ed., *Total Baseball*. 6th ed. New York: Total Sports, Inc., 1999.

Trainor, Jim, *The Complete Baseball Play Book*. New York: Doubleday and Co., 1972.

Verducci, Tom, "An Armful," *Sports Illustrated*, 87, 1 (July 7, 1997).

Verducci, Tom, "Triple Threats," *Sports Illustrated*, 85, 1 (July 1, 1996).

Voigt, David Quentin, *Baseball: An Illustrated History*. University Park: Pennsylvania State University Press, 1987.

Wallop, Douglas, *Baseball: An Informal History*. New York: W. W. Norton, 1969.

Ward, John Montgomery, *Base-ball: How to Become a Player, with the Origin, History, and Explanation of the Game*. Cleveland, Ohio: Society for American Baseball Research, 1993. [orig. publ. 1888].

Weaver, Earl, with Berry Stainback, *It's What You Learn After You Know It All That Counts*. Garden City, N.Y.: Doubleday and Co., 1982.

Will, George F., *Men at Work: The Craft of Baseball*. New York: Macmillan Publishing Co., 1990.

Williams, Peter, *When the Giants Were Giants: Bill Terry and the Golden Age of New York Baseball*. Chapel Hill, N.C.: Algonquin Books of Chapel Hill, 1994.

Williams, Peter, ed., *The Joe Williams Baseball Reader*. Chapel Hill, N.C.: Algonquin Books of Chapel Hill, 1989.

Williams, Ted, "It's Time to Open the Door," *The National Pastime: A Review of Baseball History*, No. 18 (1998).

Williams, Ted, with John Underwood, *The Science of Hitting*. New York: Simon and Schuster, 1971.

Wright, Craig R., and Tom House, *The Diamond Appraised*. New York: Simon and Schuster, 1989.

Yardley, Jonathan, *Ring: A Biography of Ring Lardner*. New York: Random House, 1977.

Zinsser, William, *Spring Training*. New York: Harper and Row, 1989.

INDEX

FOL

APR - 9 2024